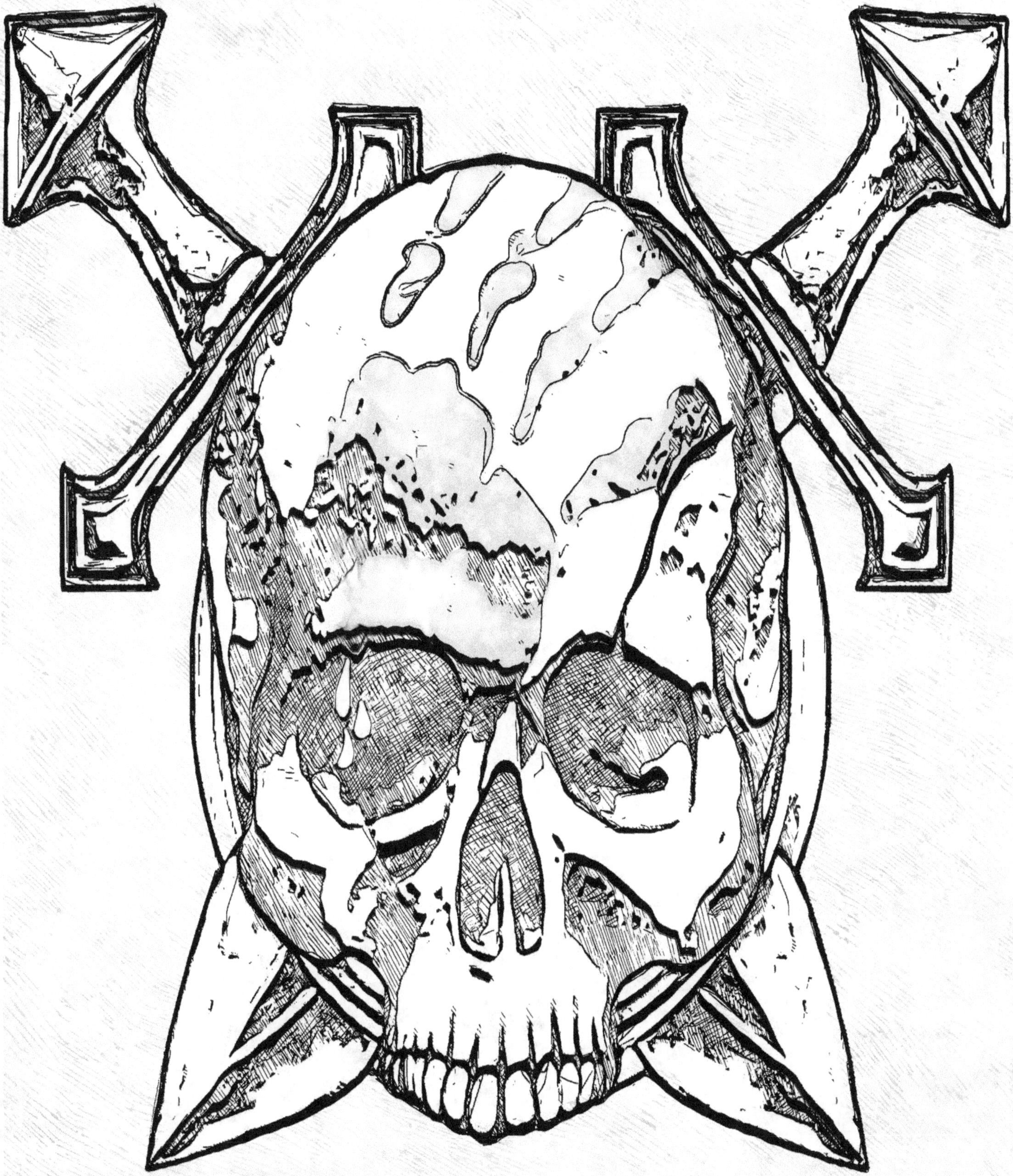

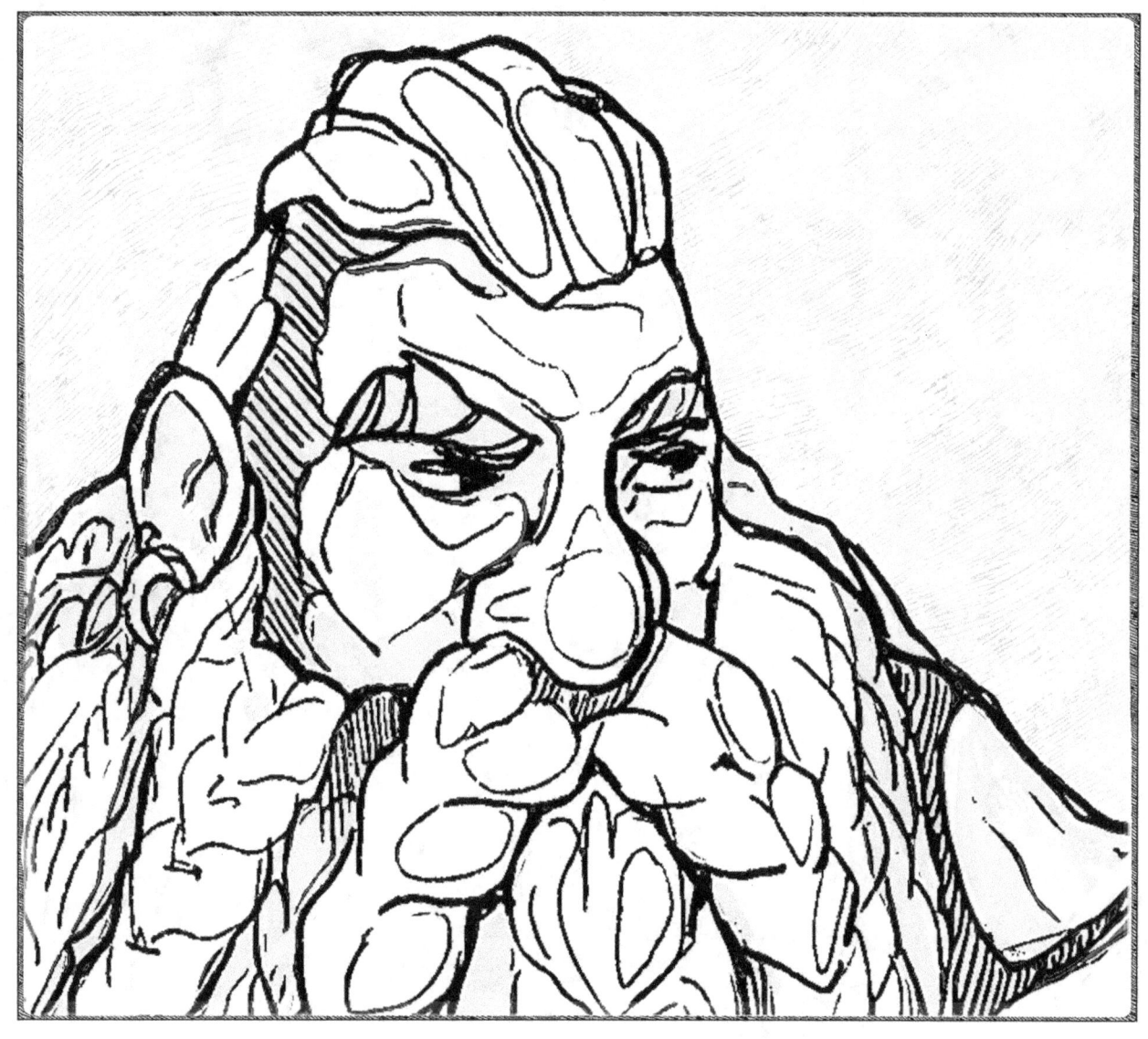

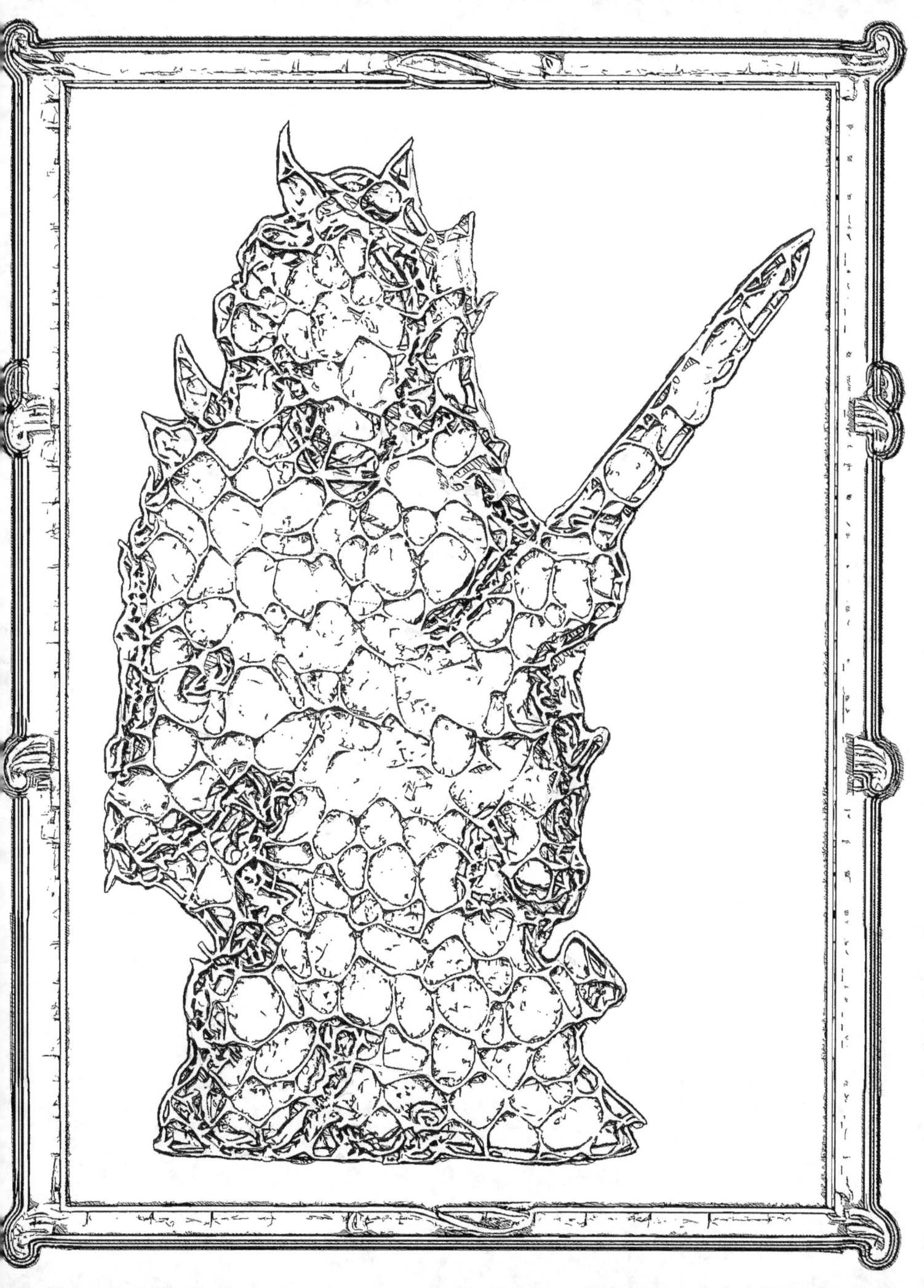

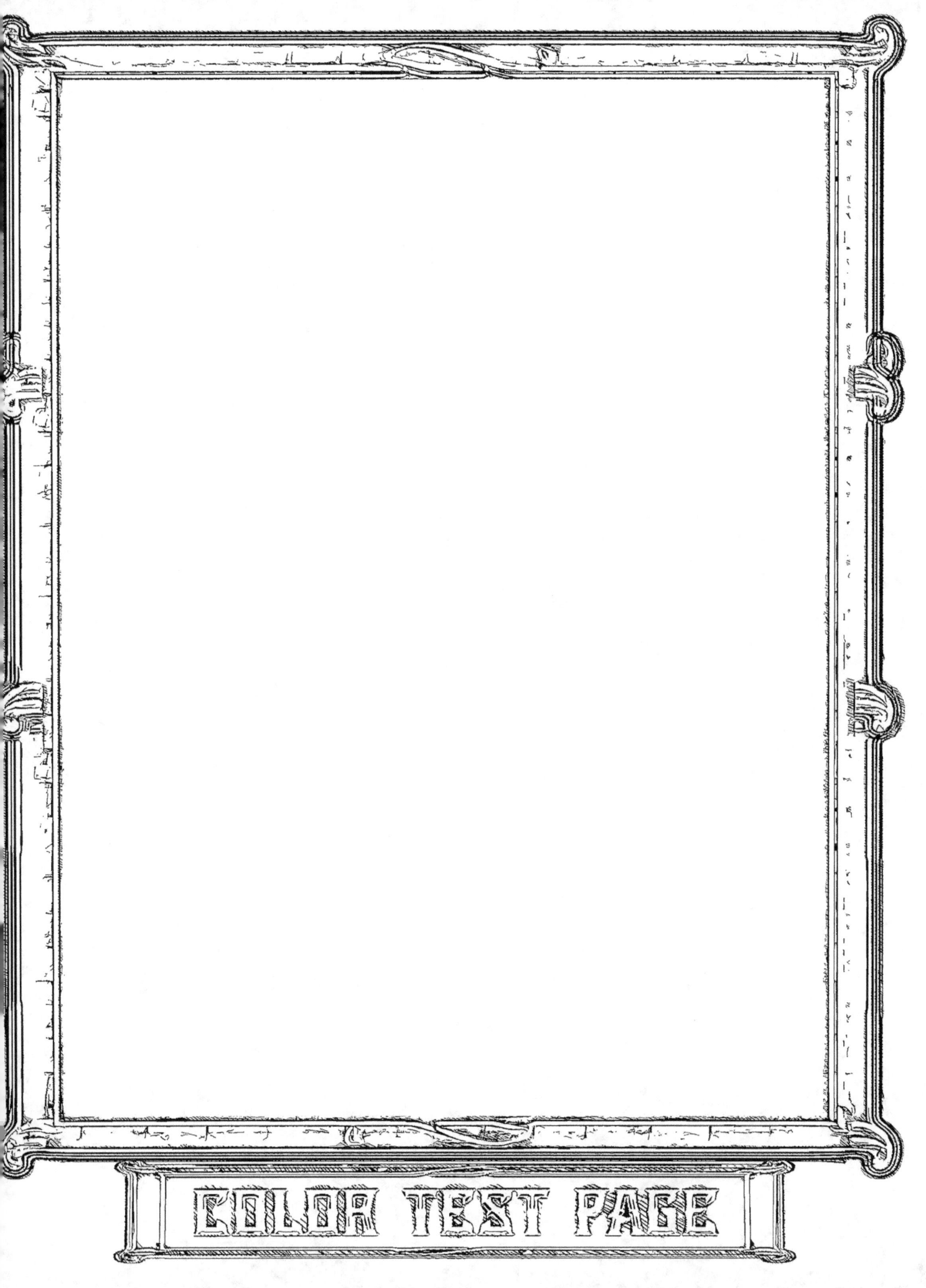

COLOR TEST PAGE

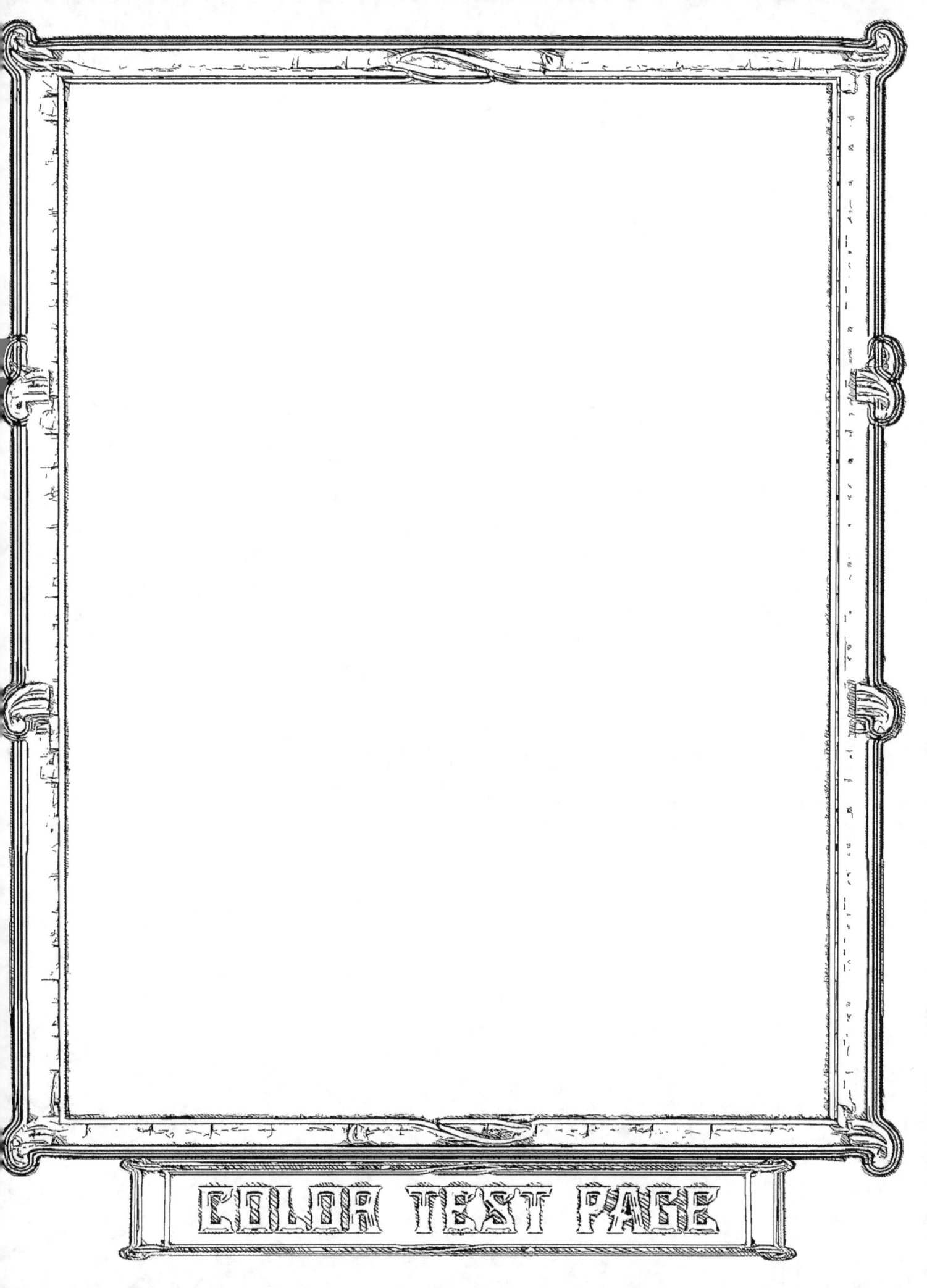

COLOR TEST PAGE

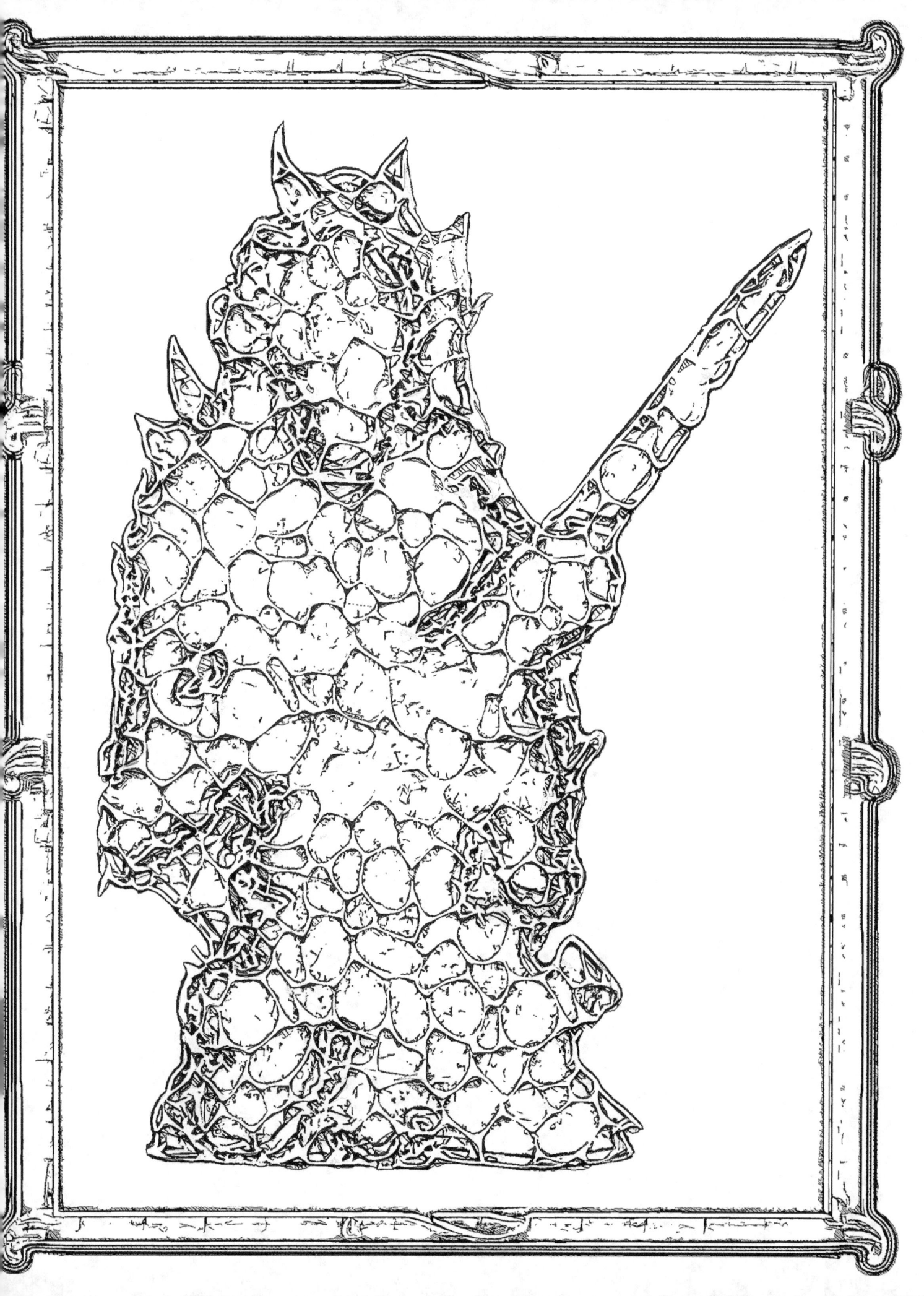

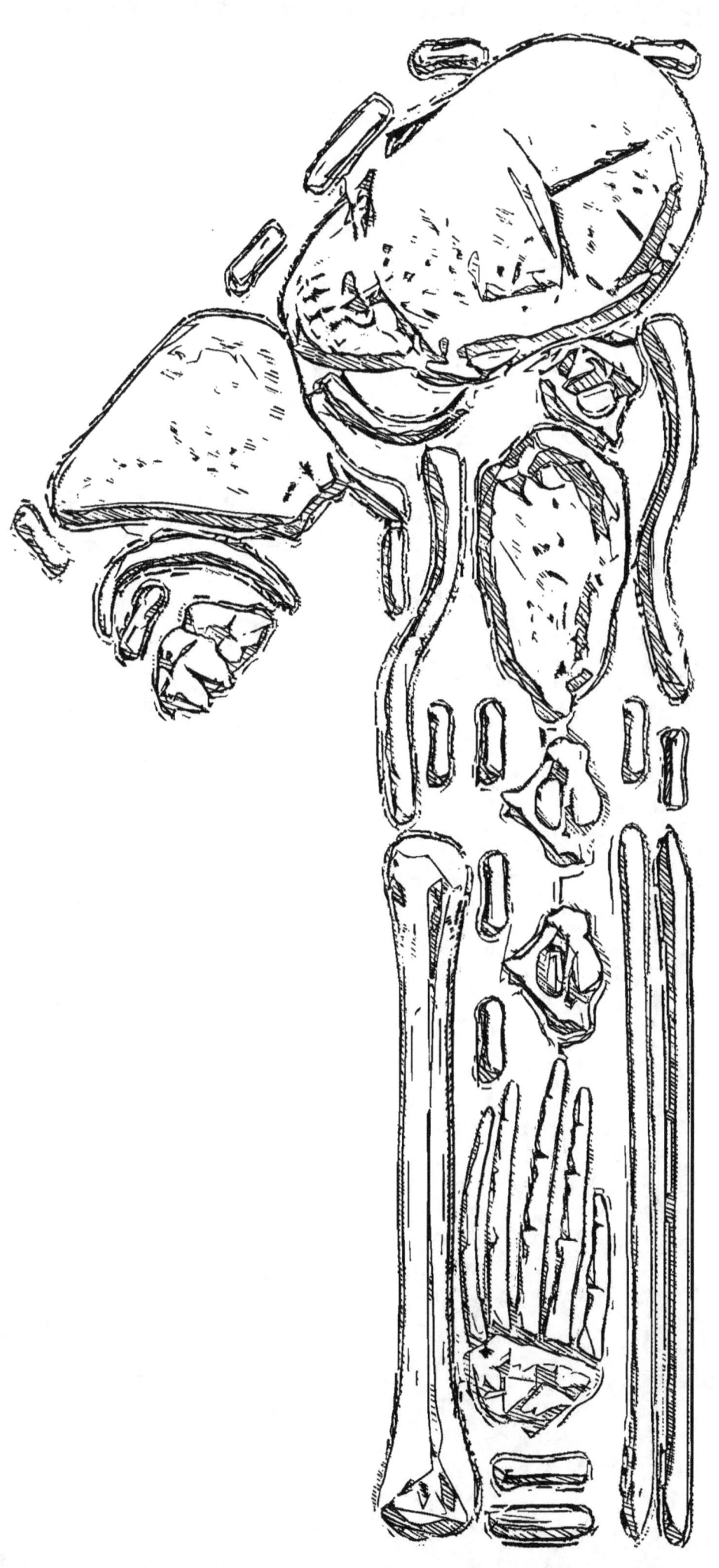

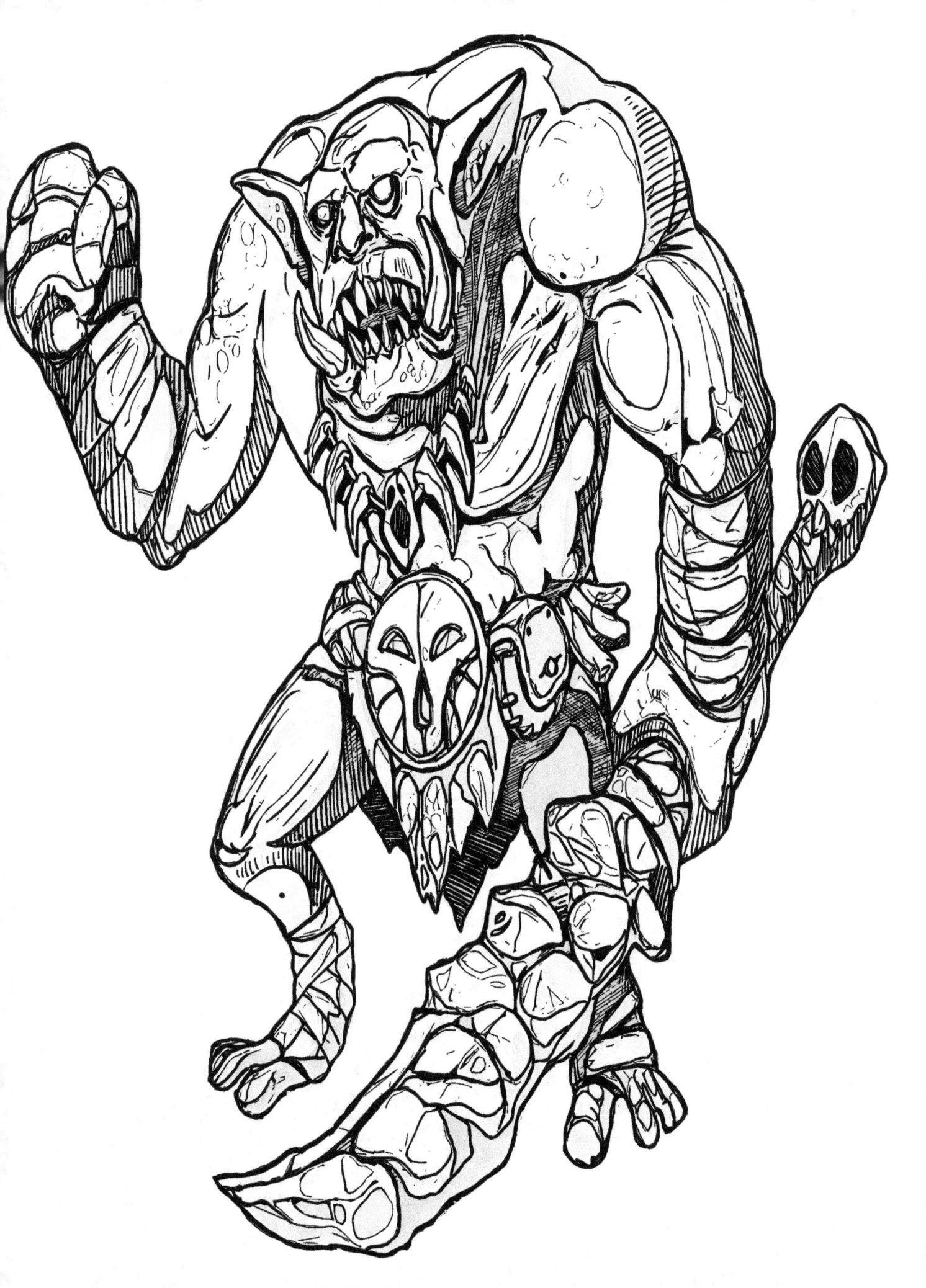

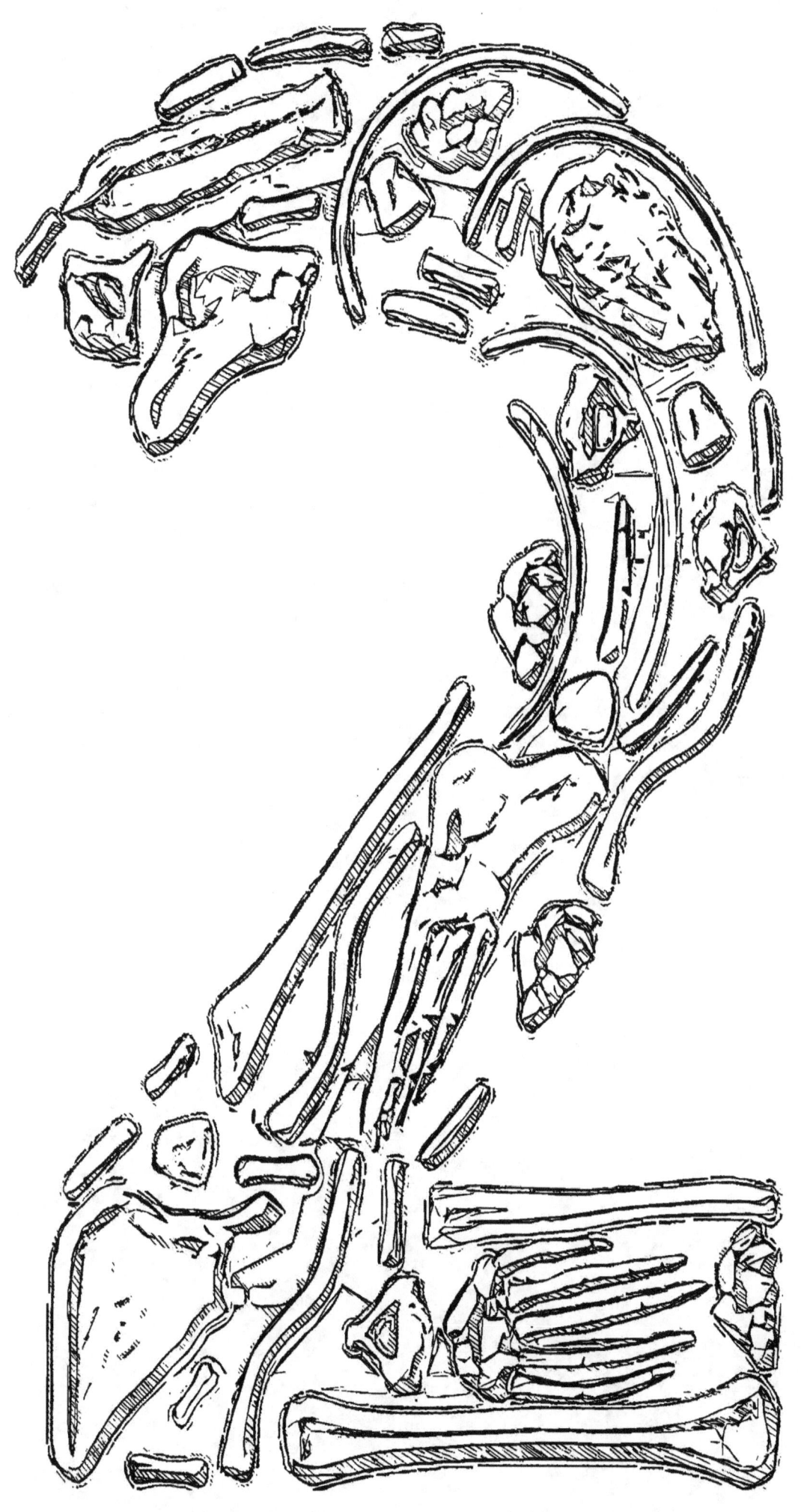

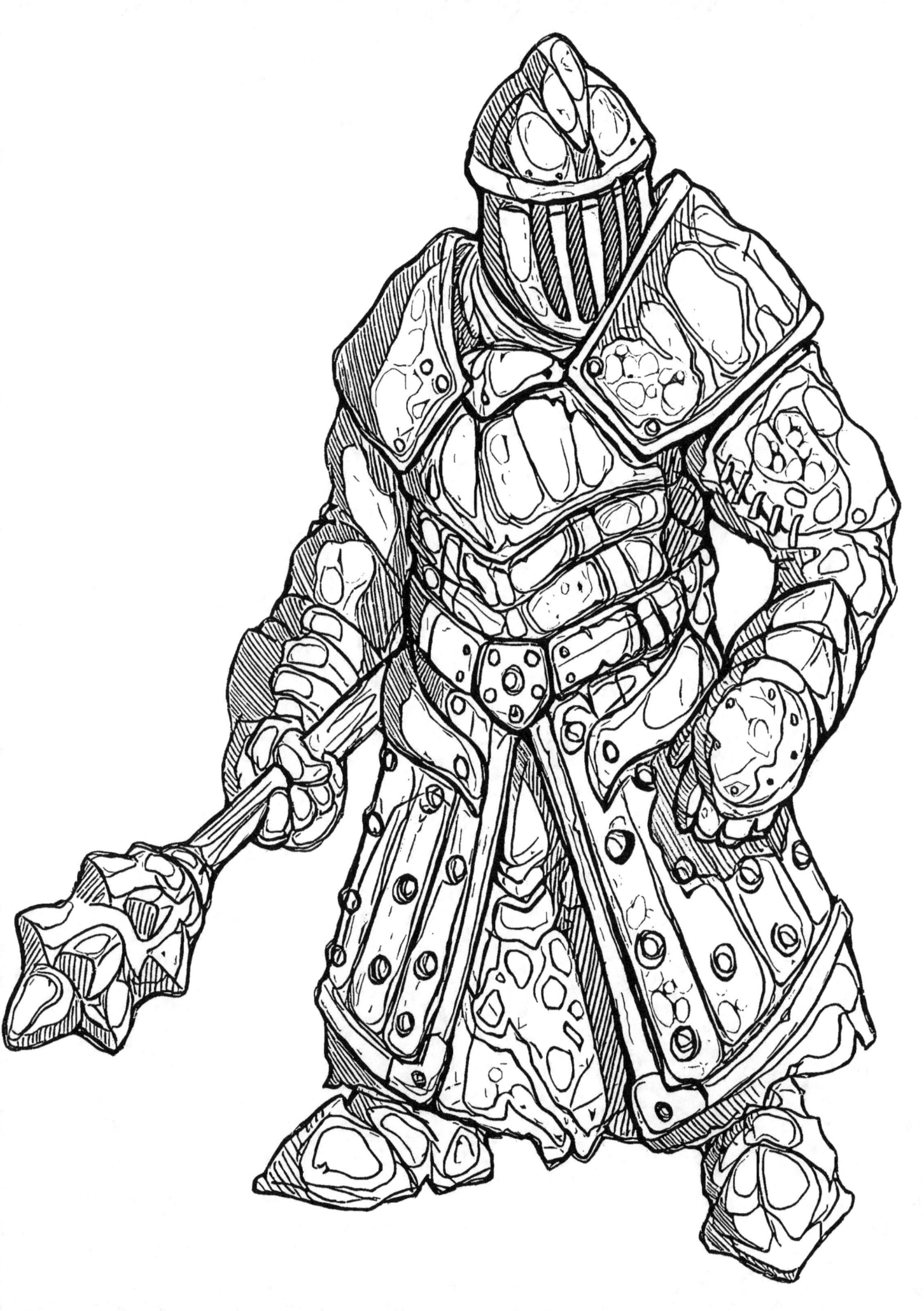

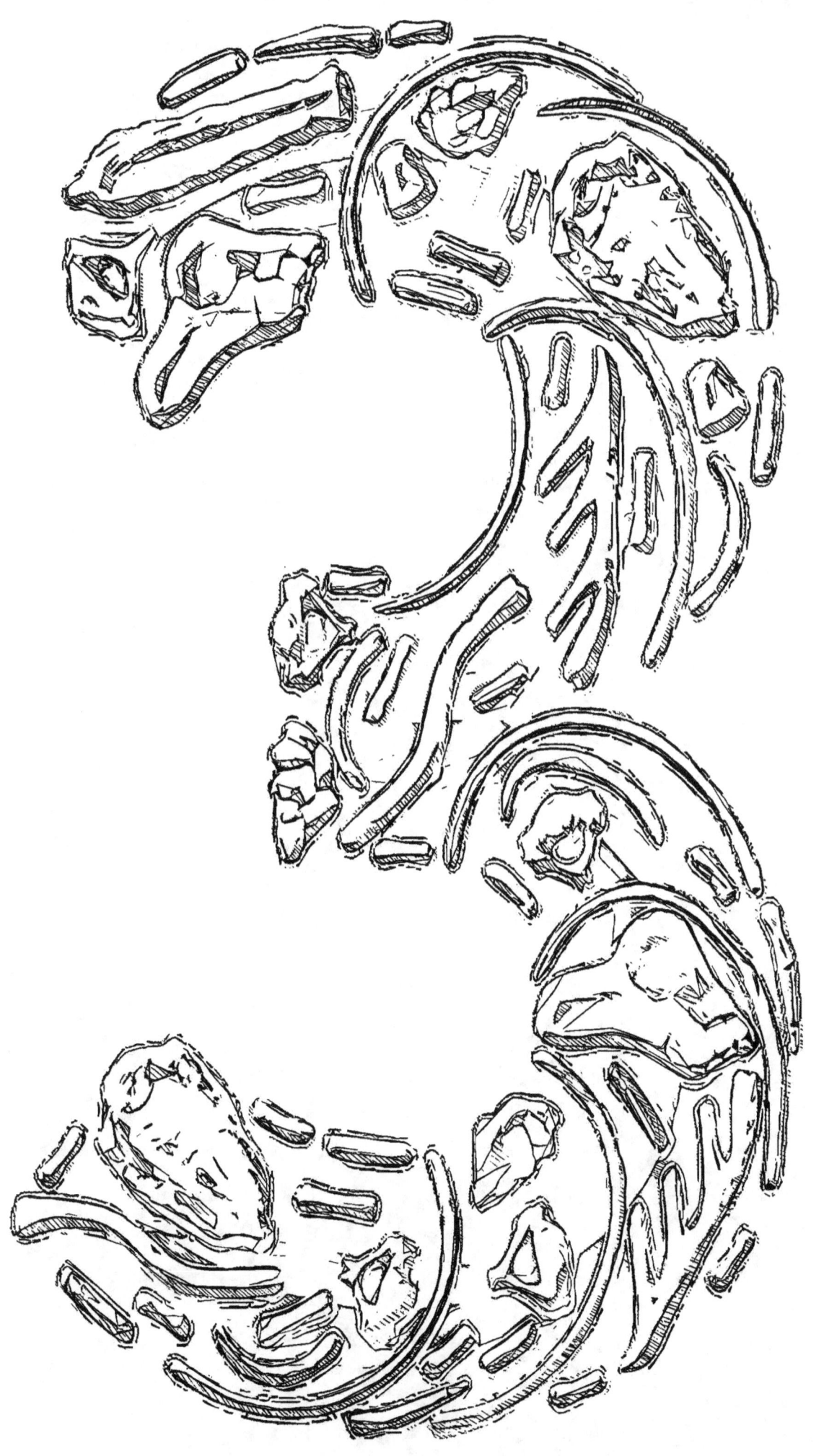

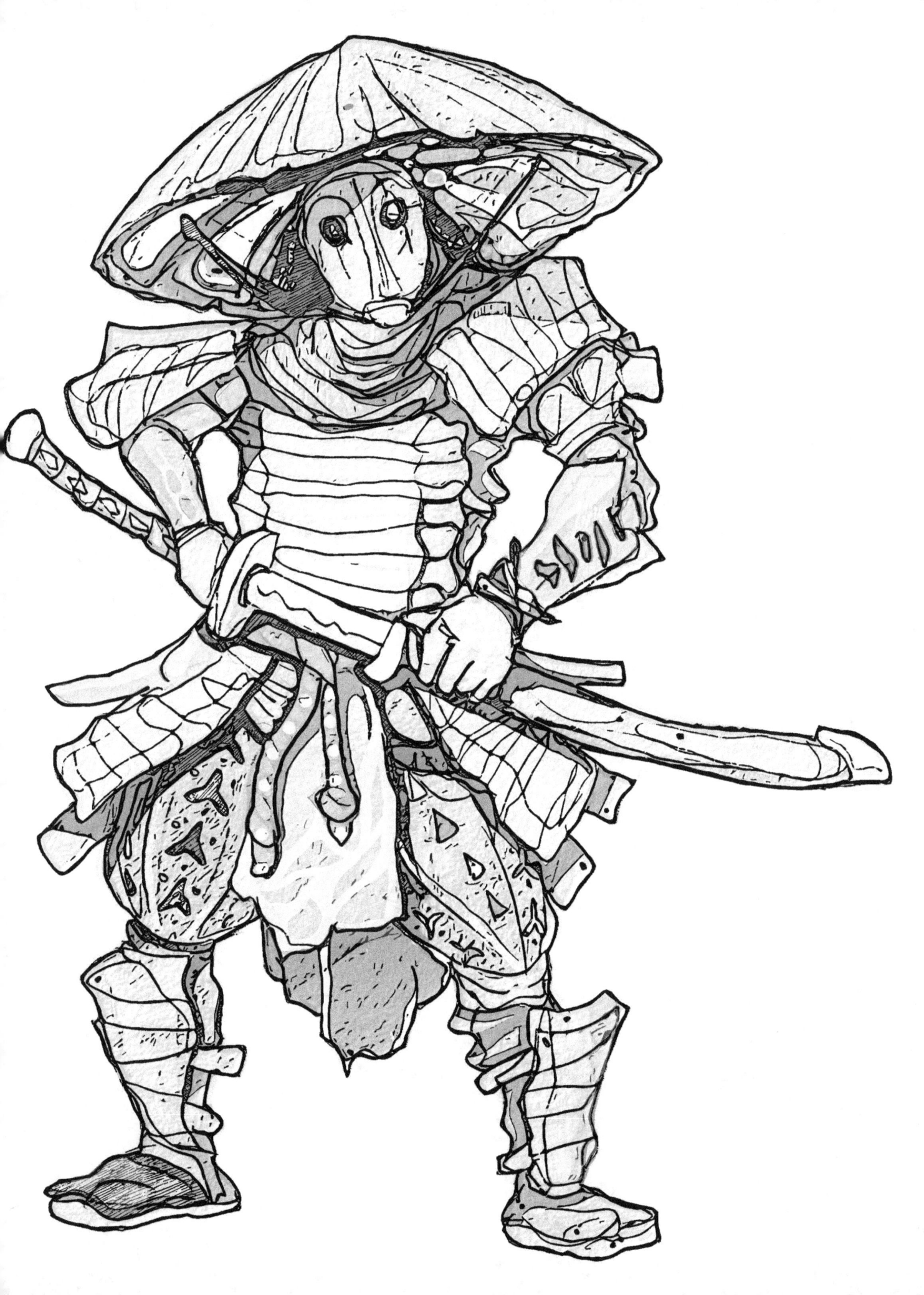

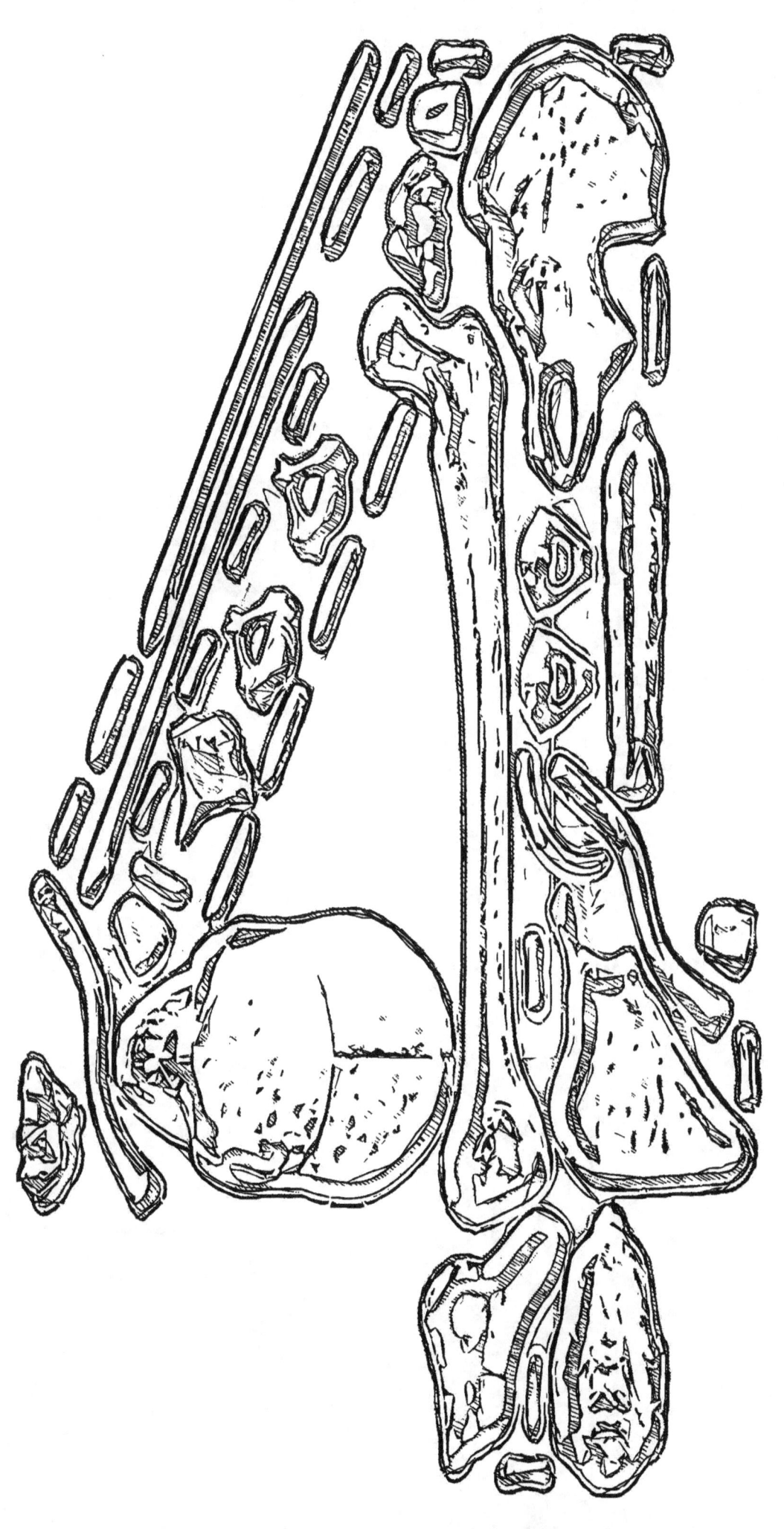

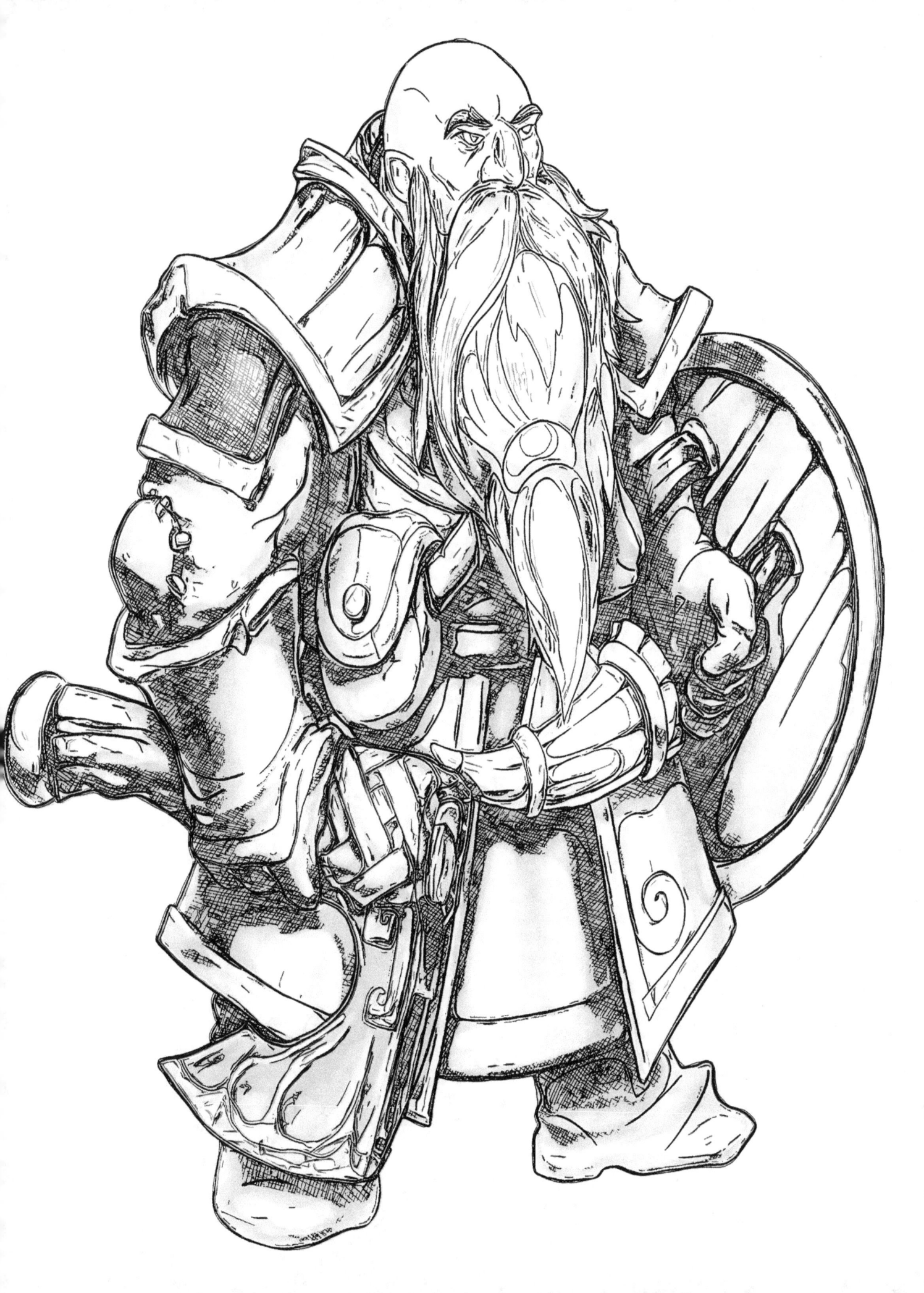

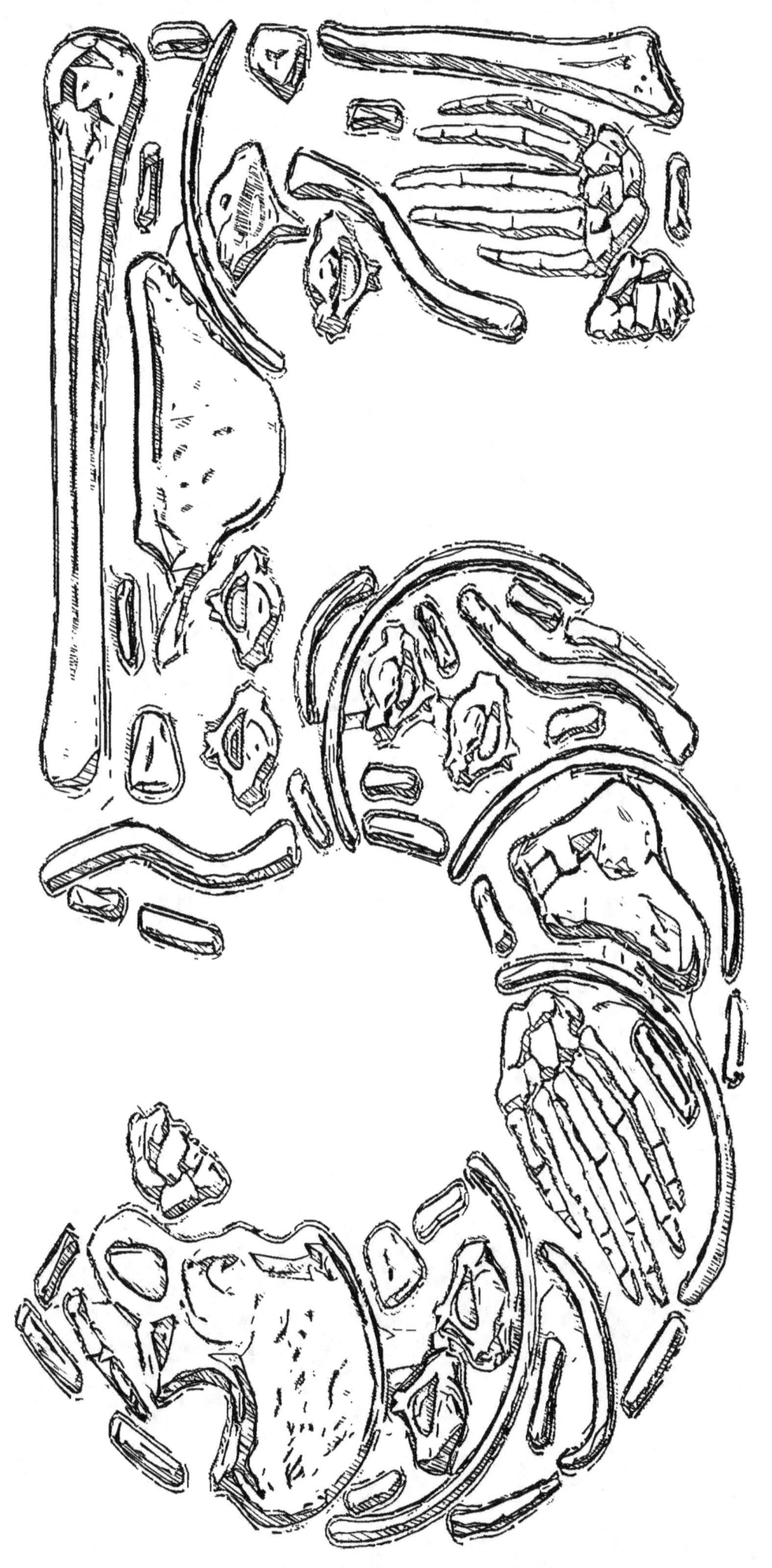

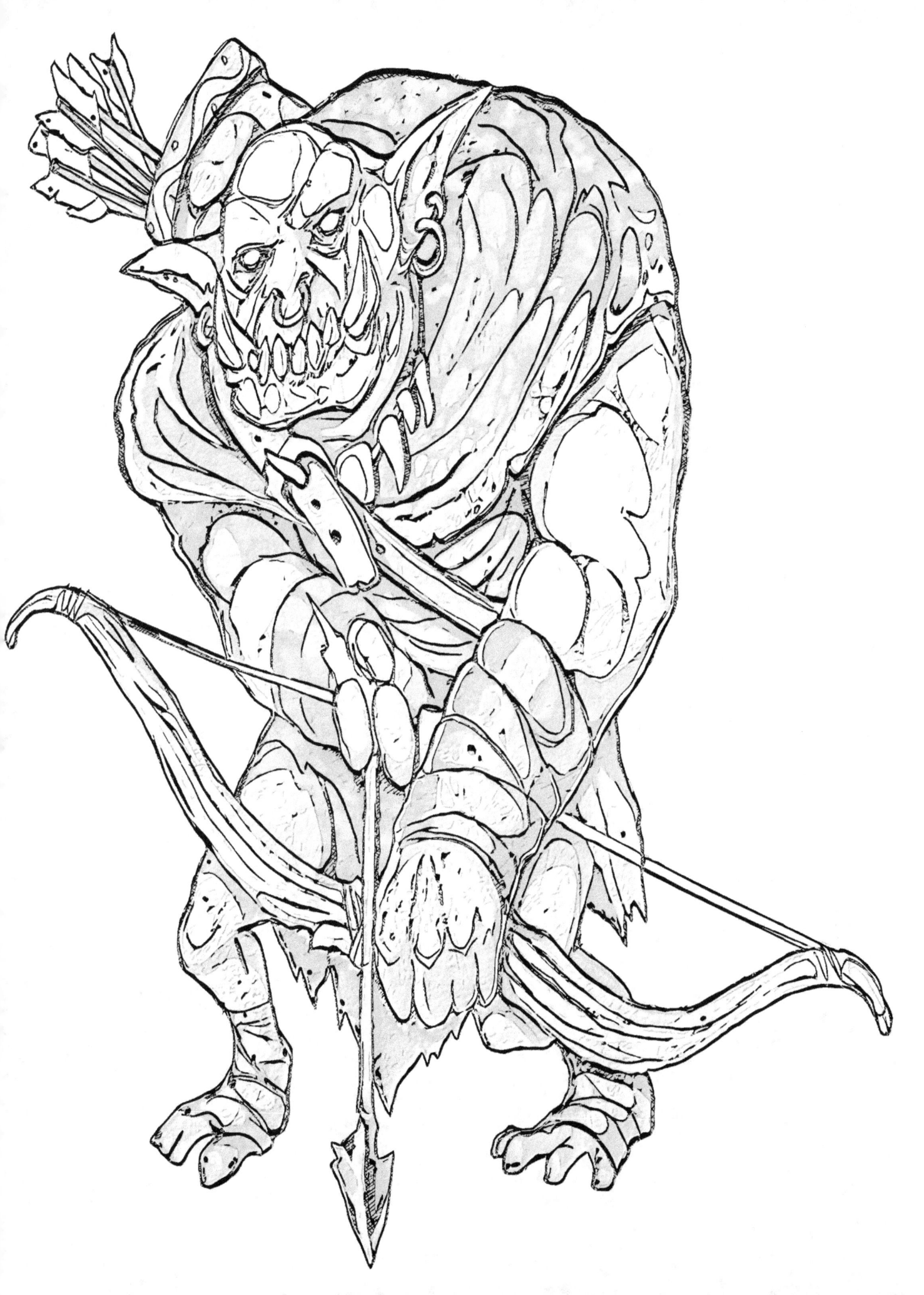

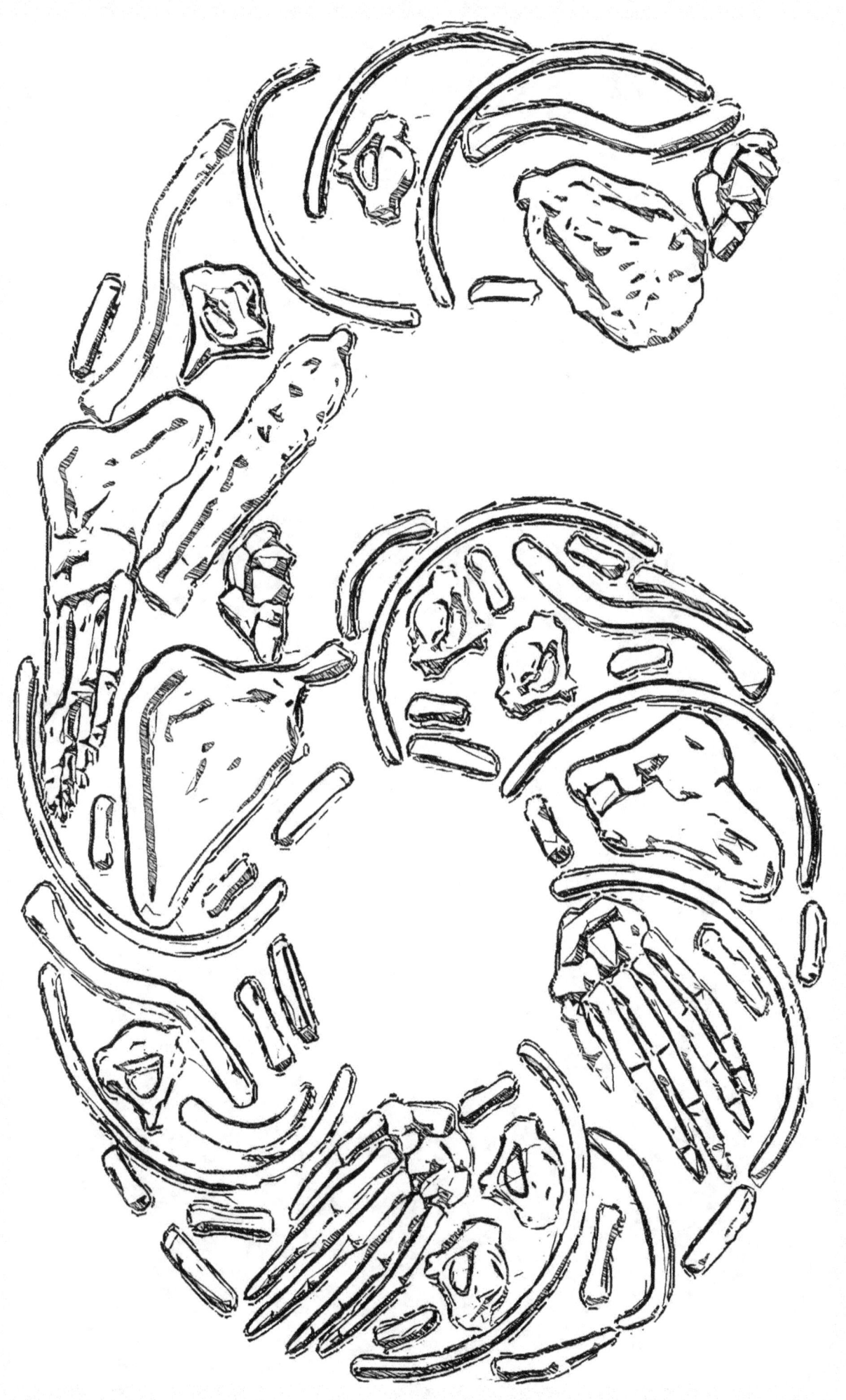

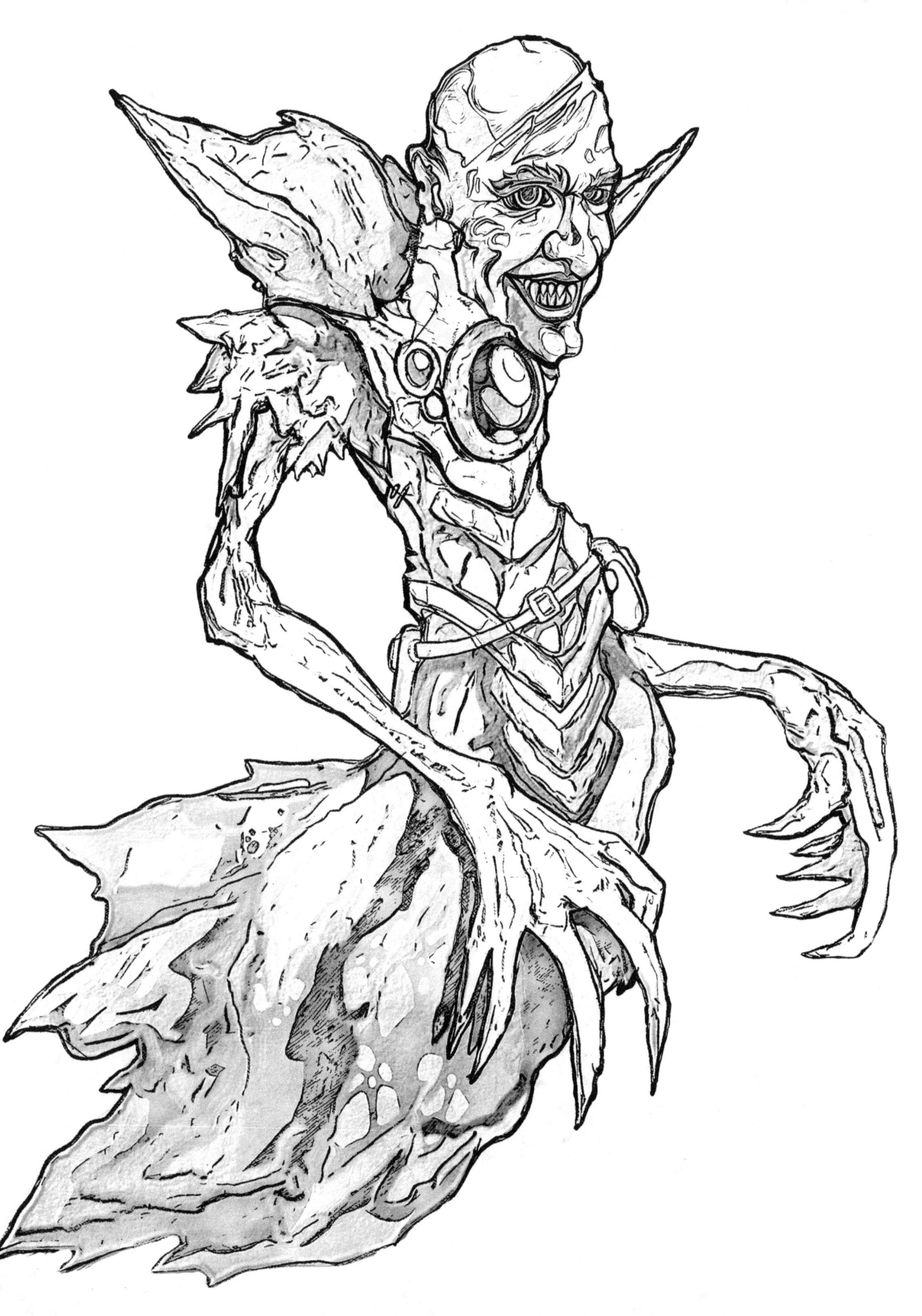

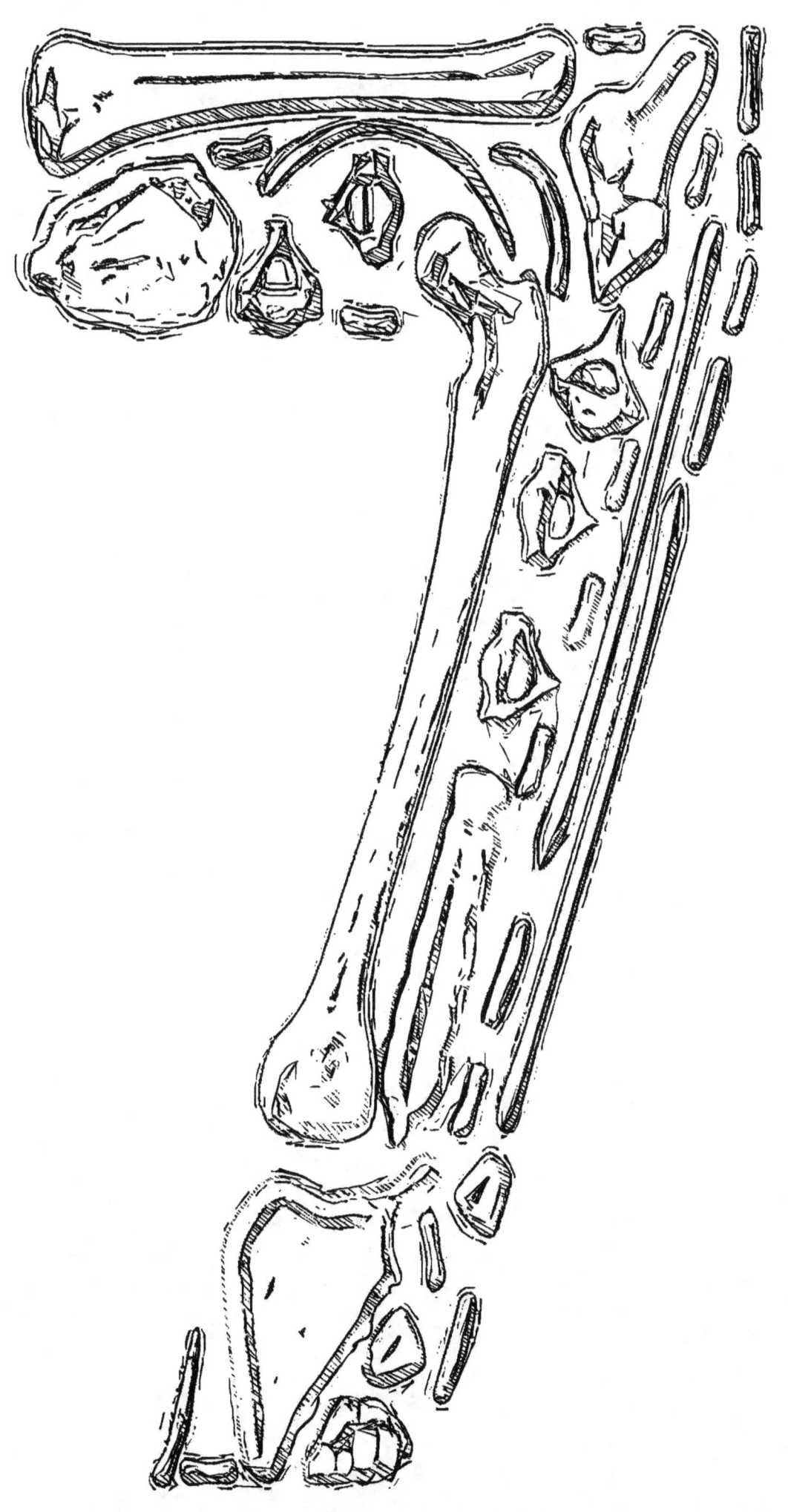

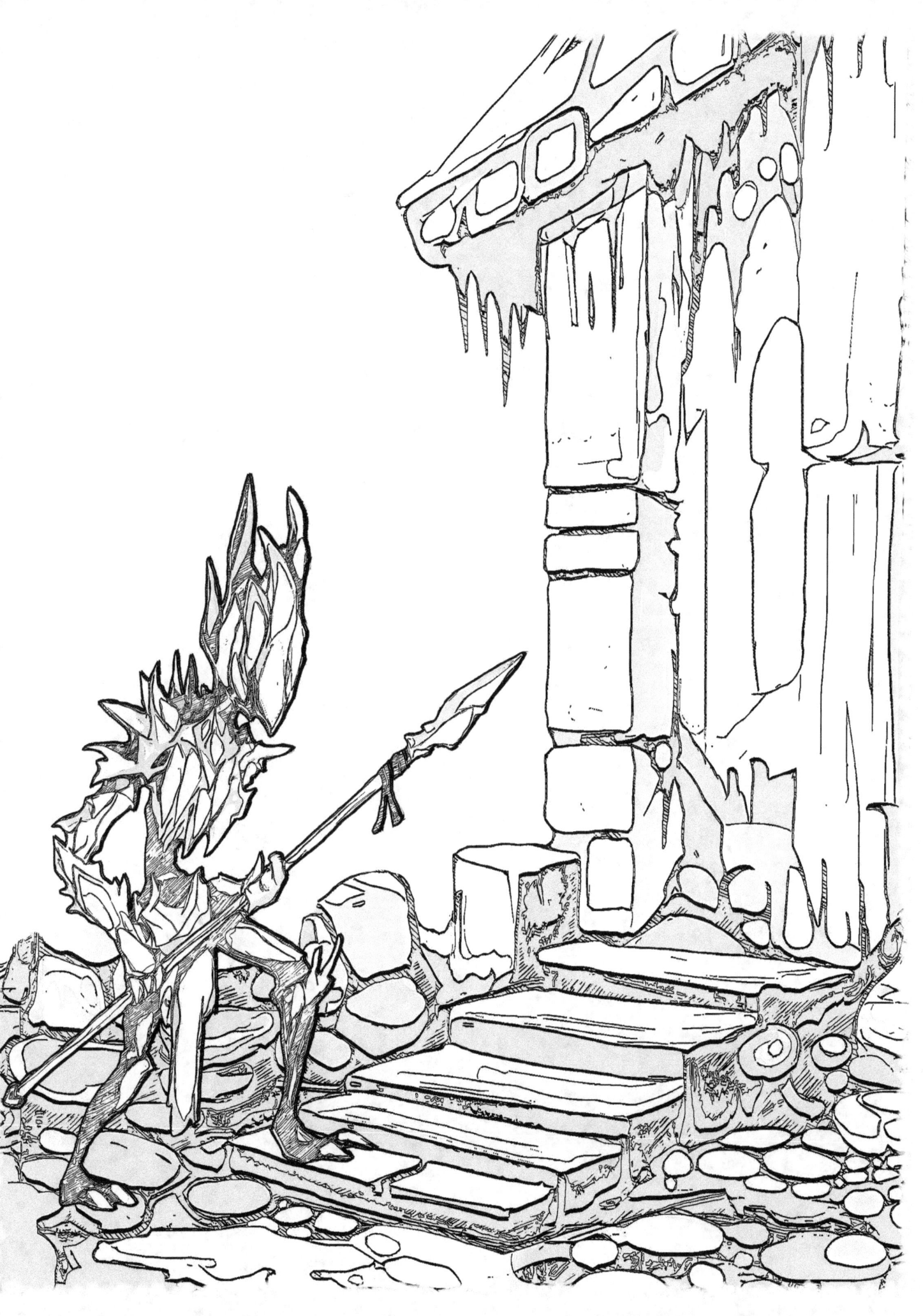

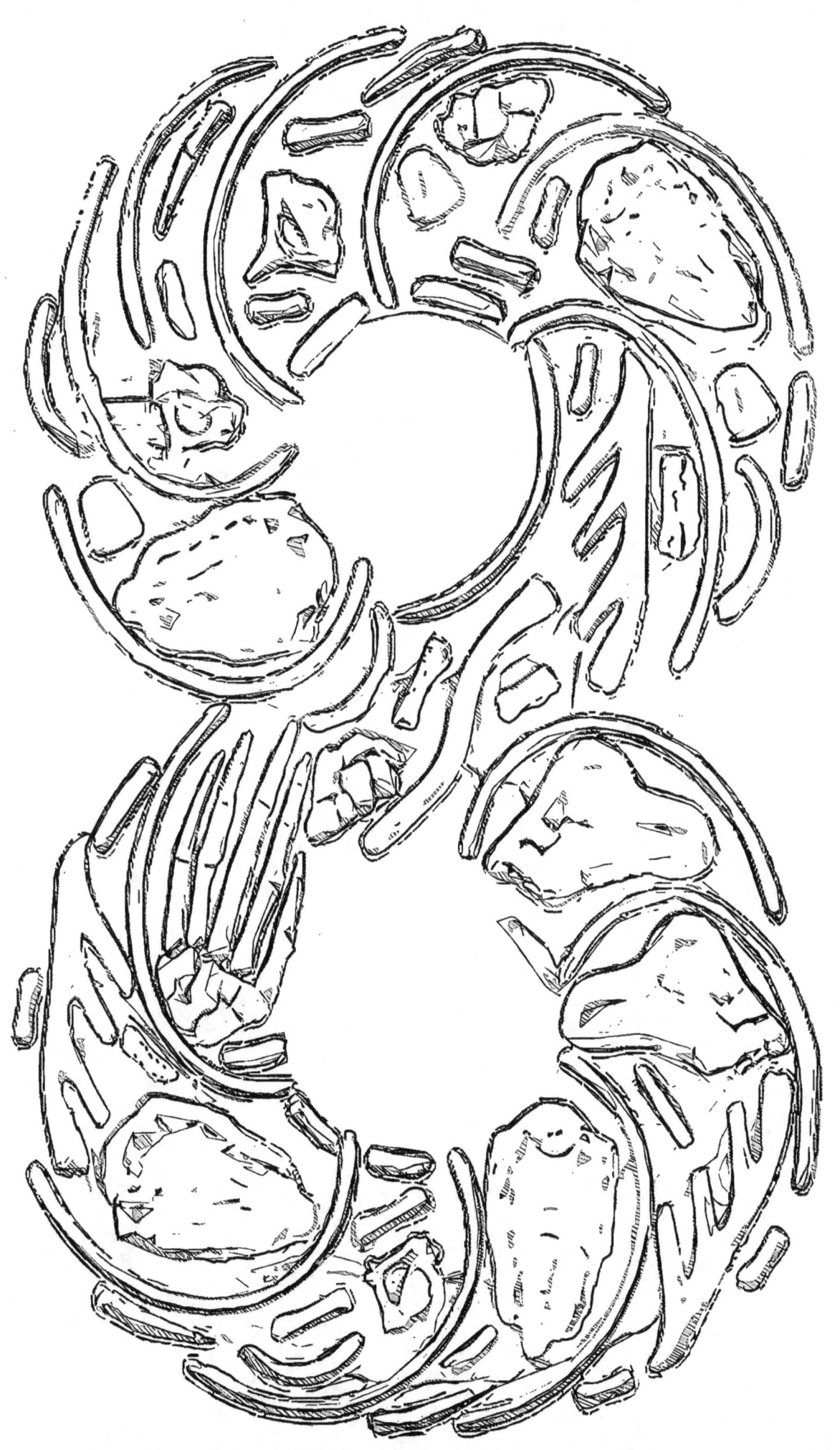

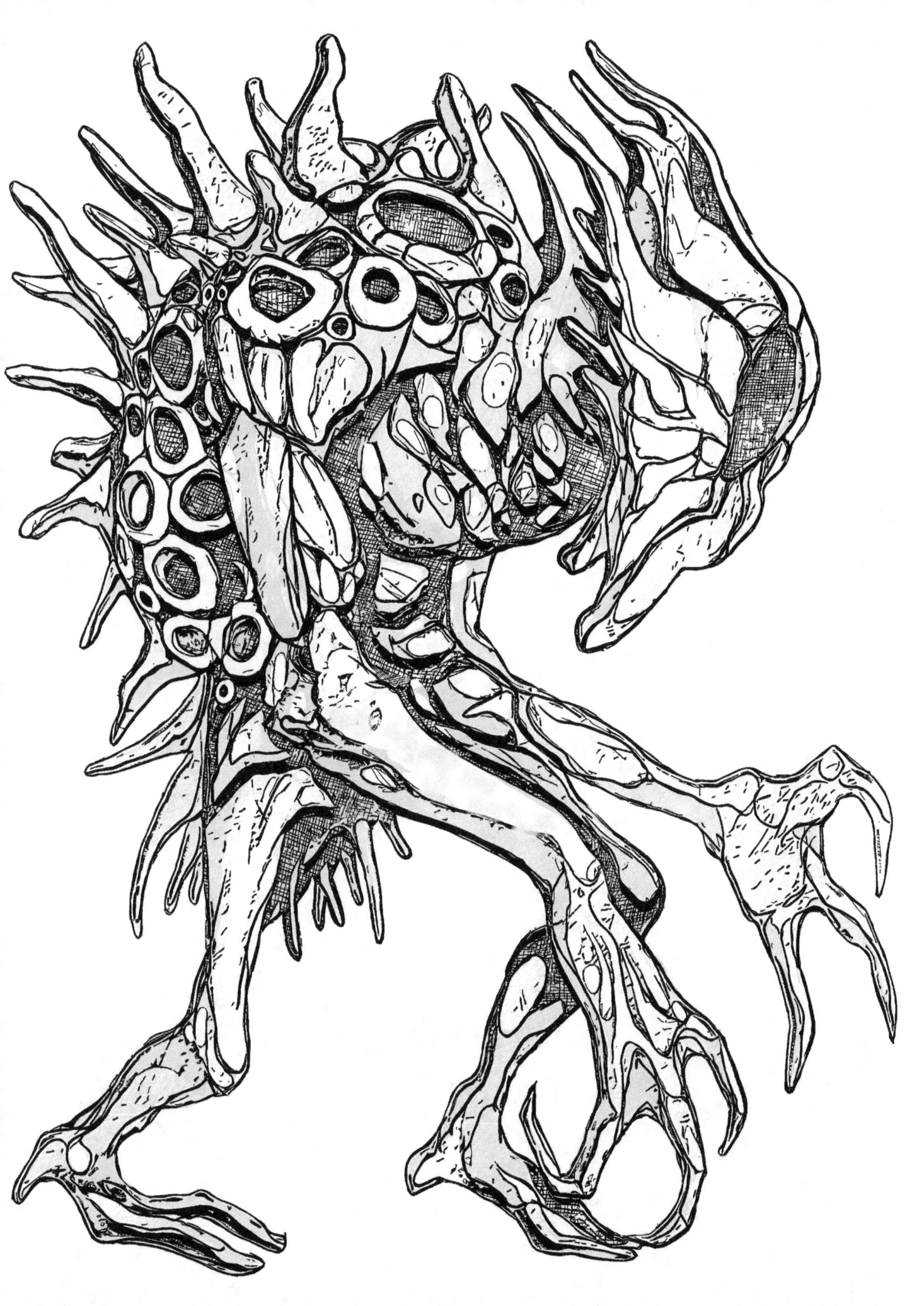

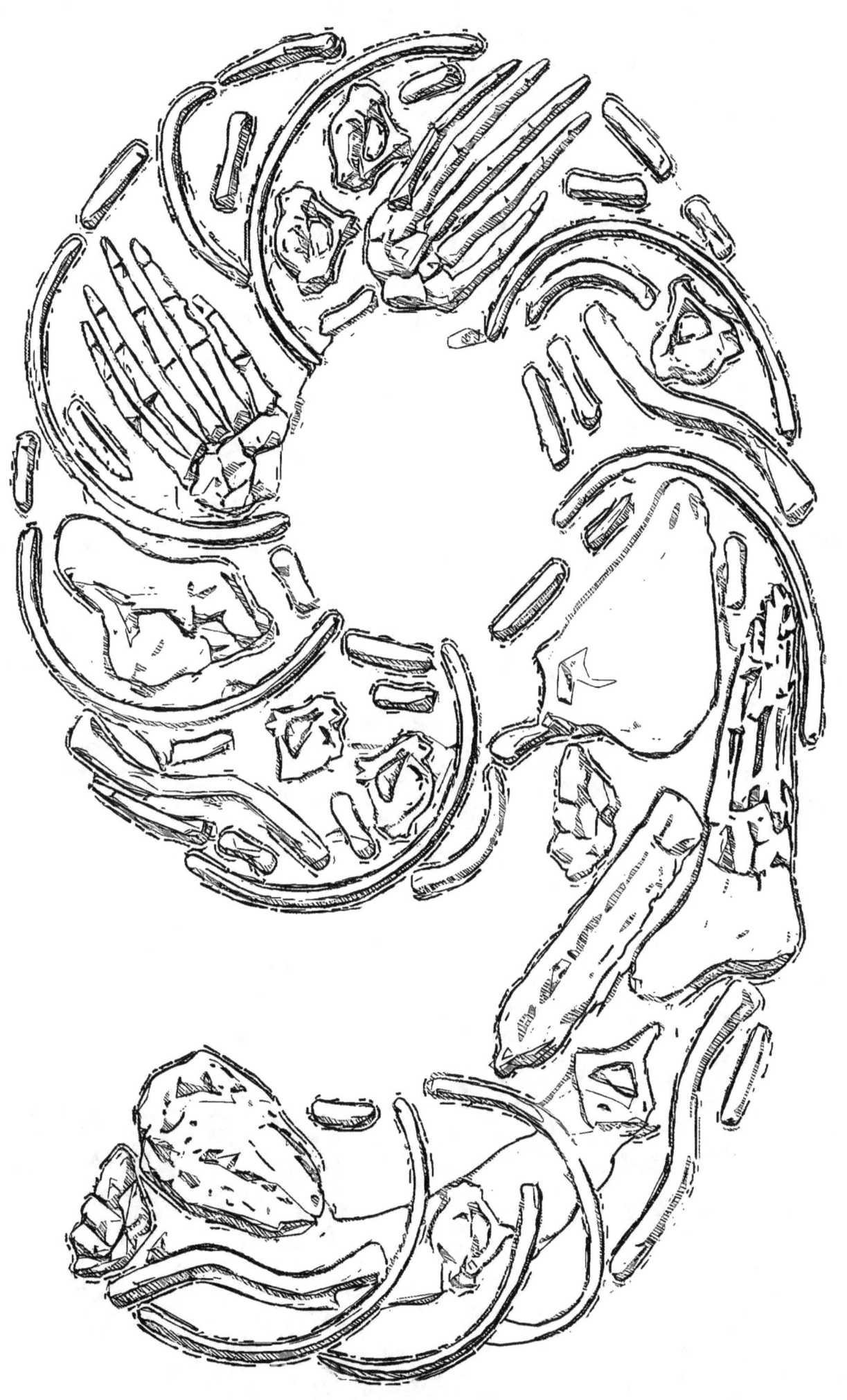

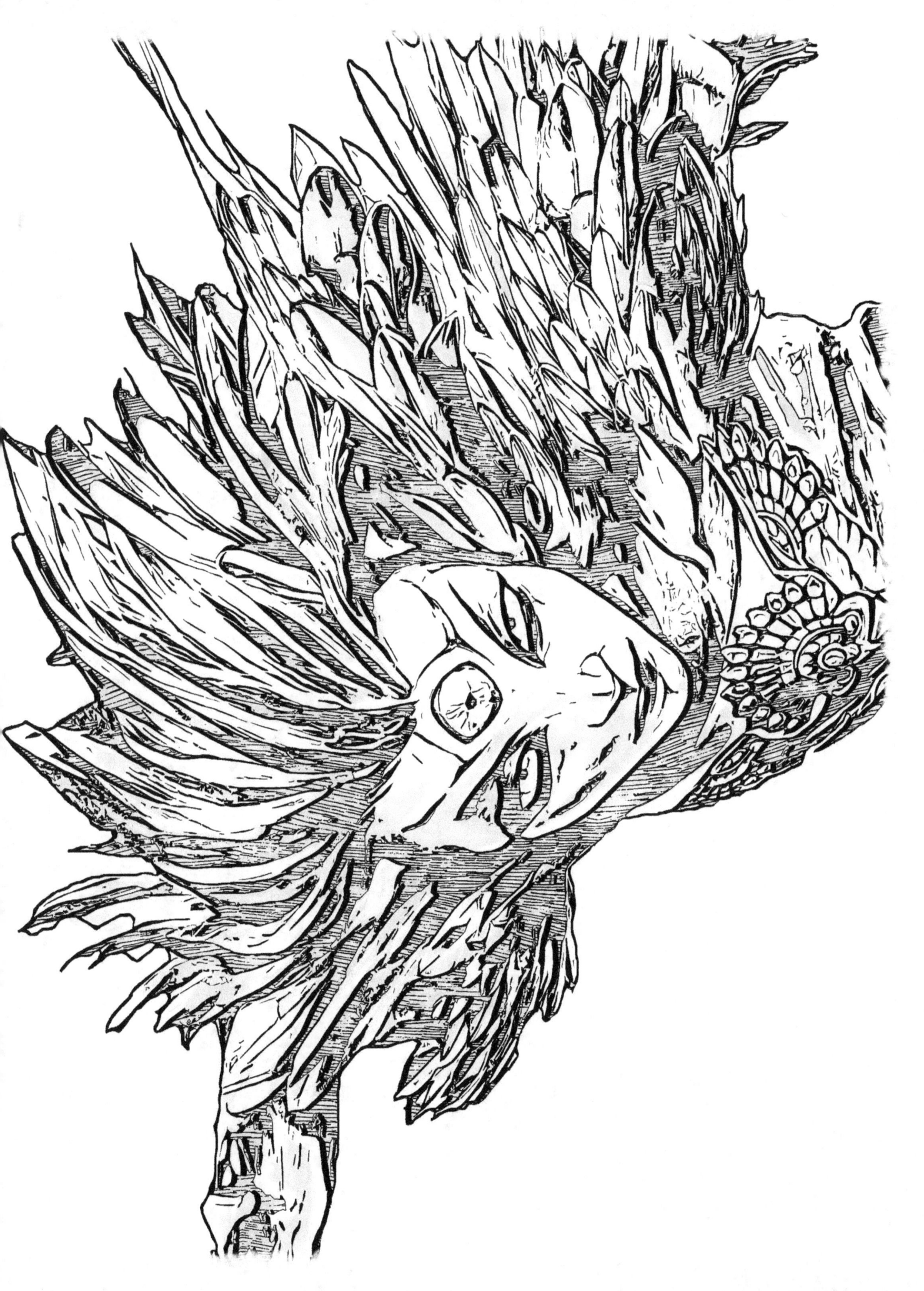

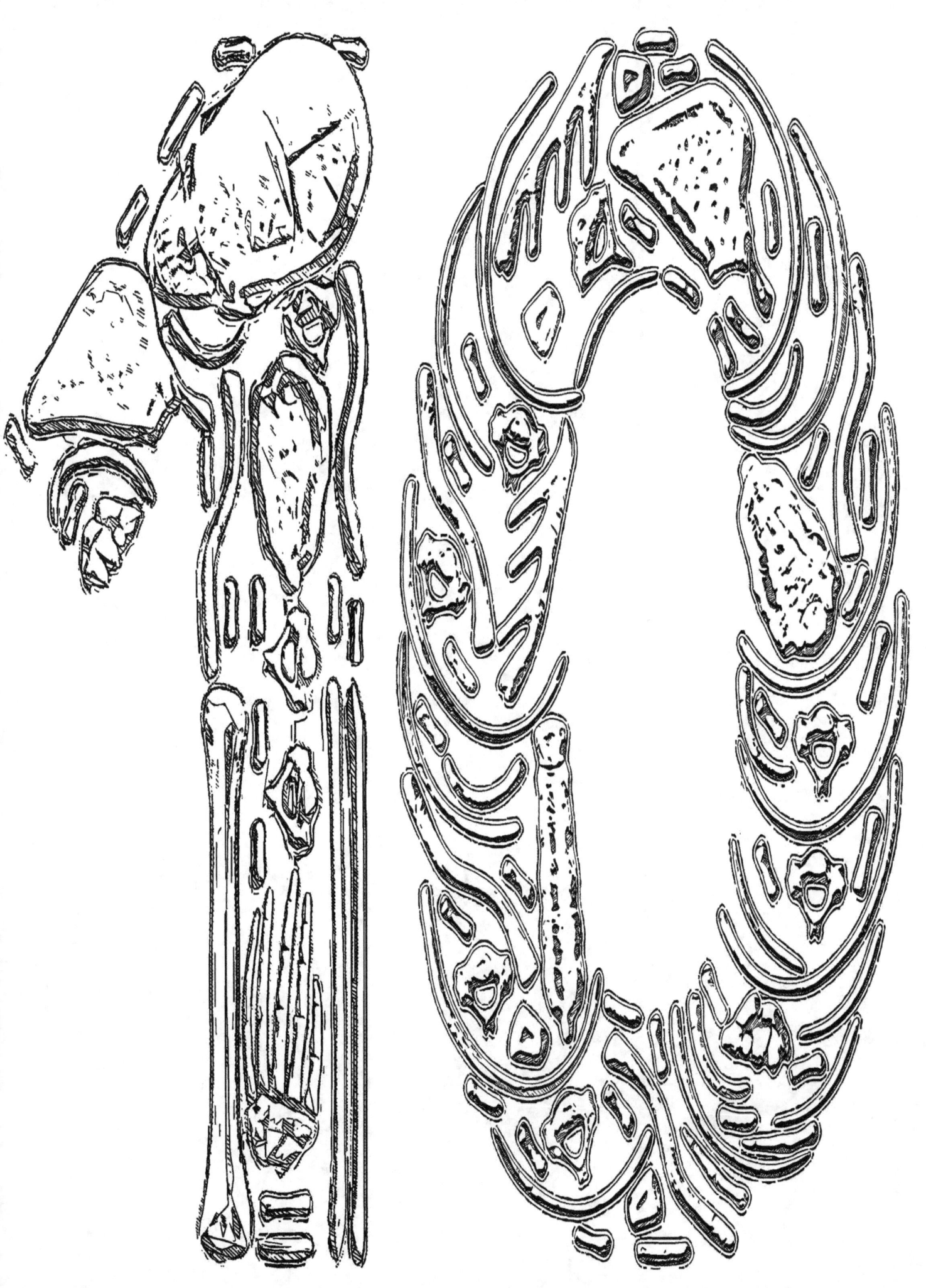

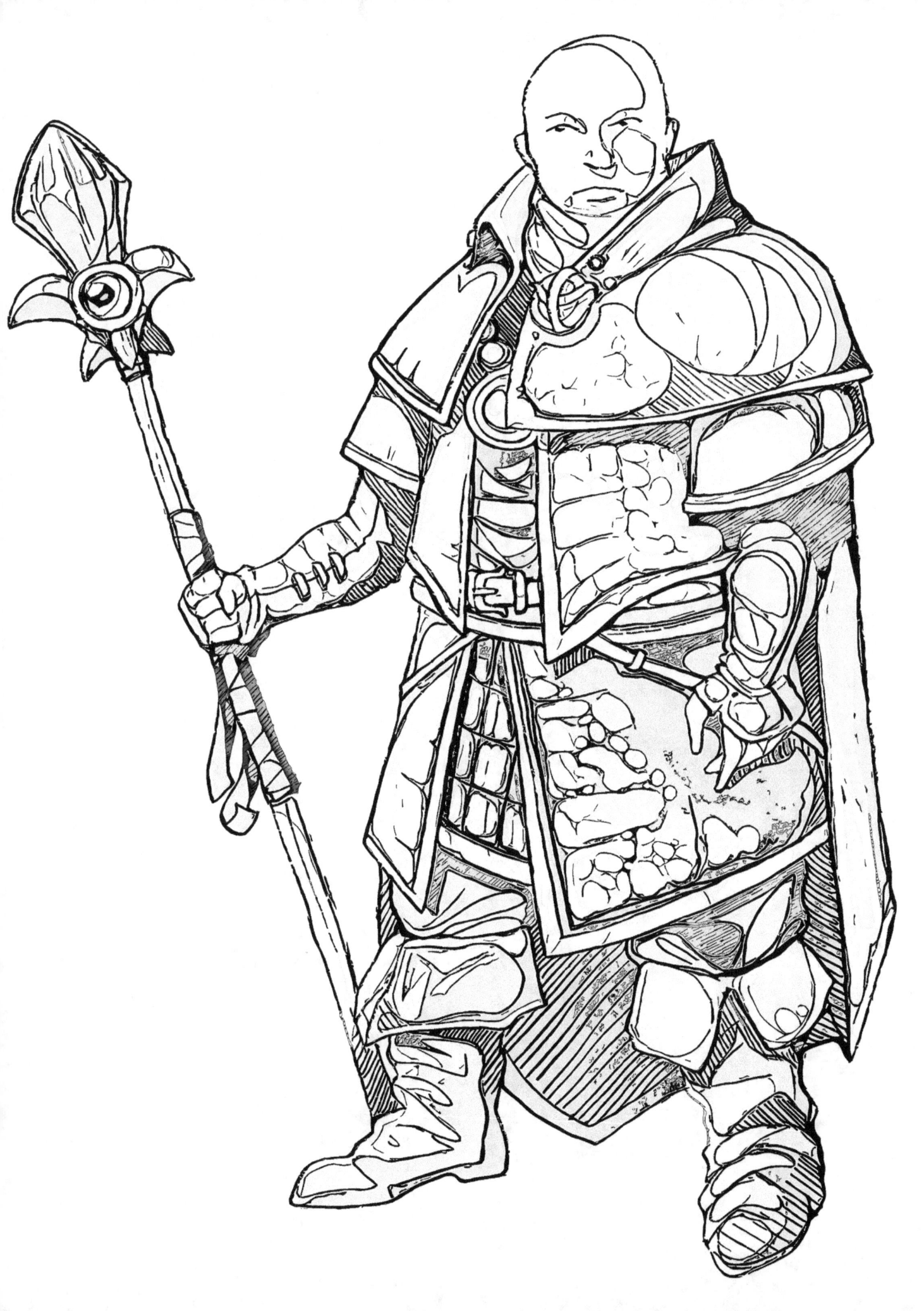

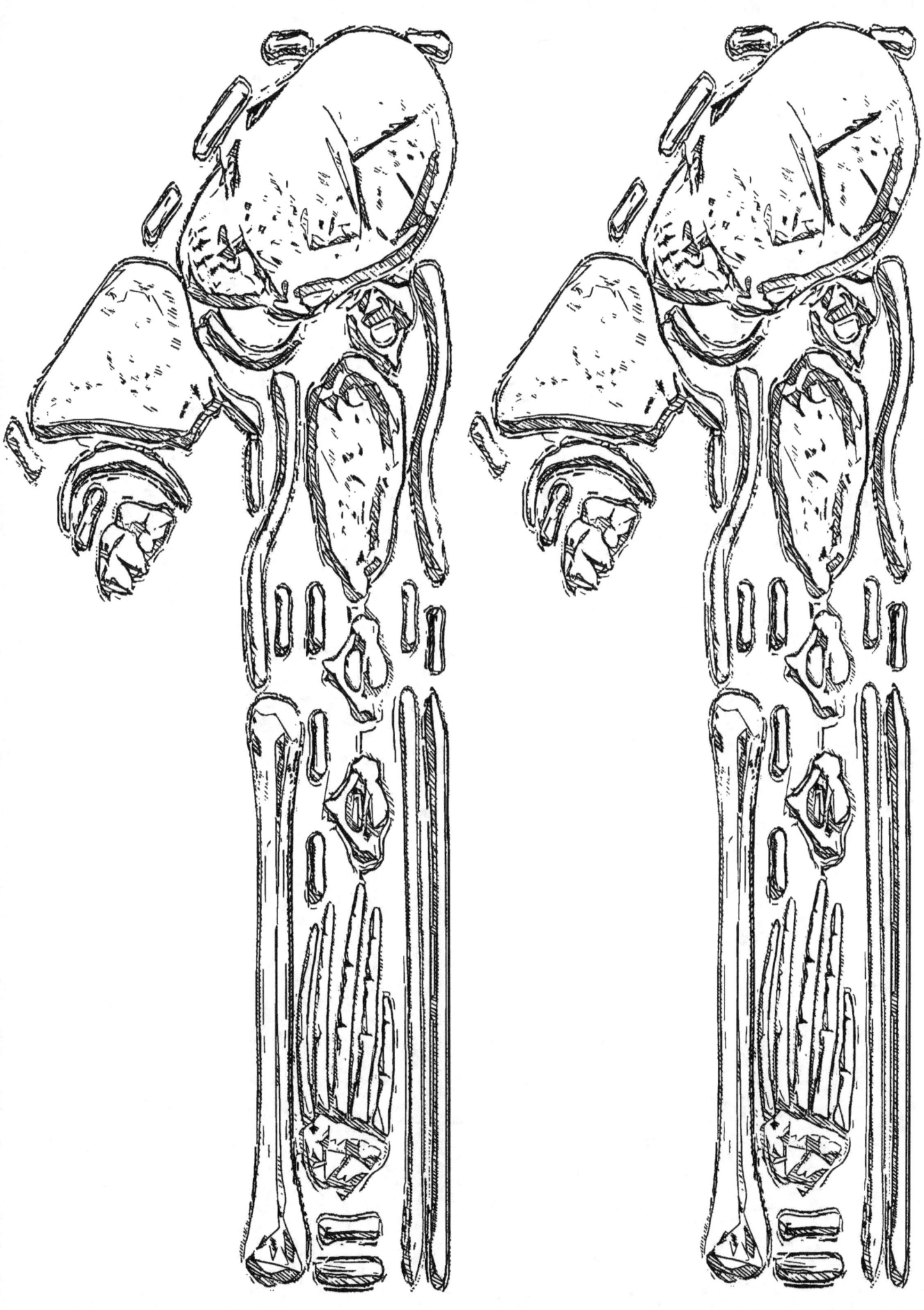

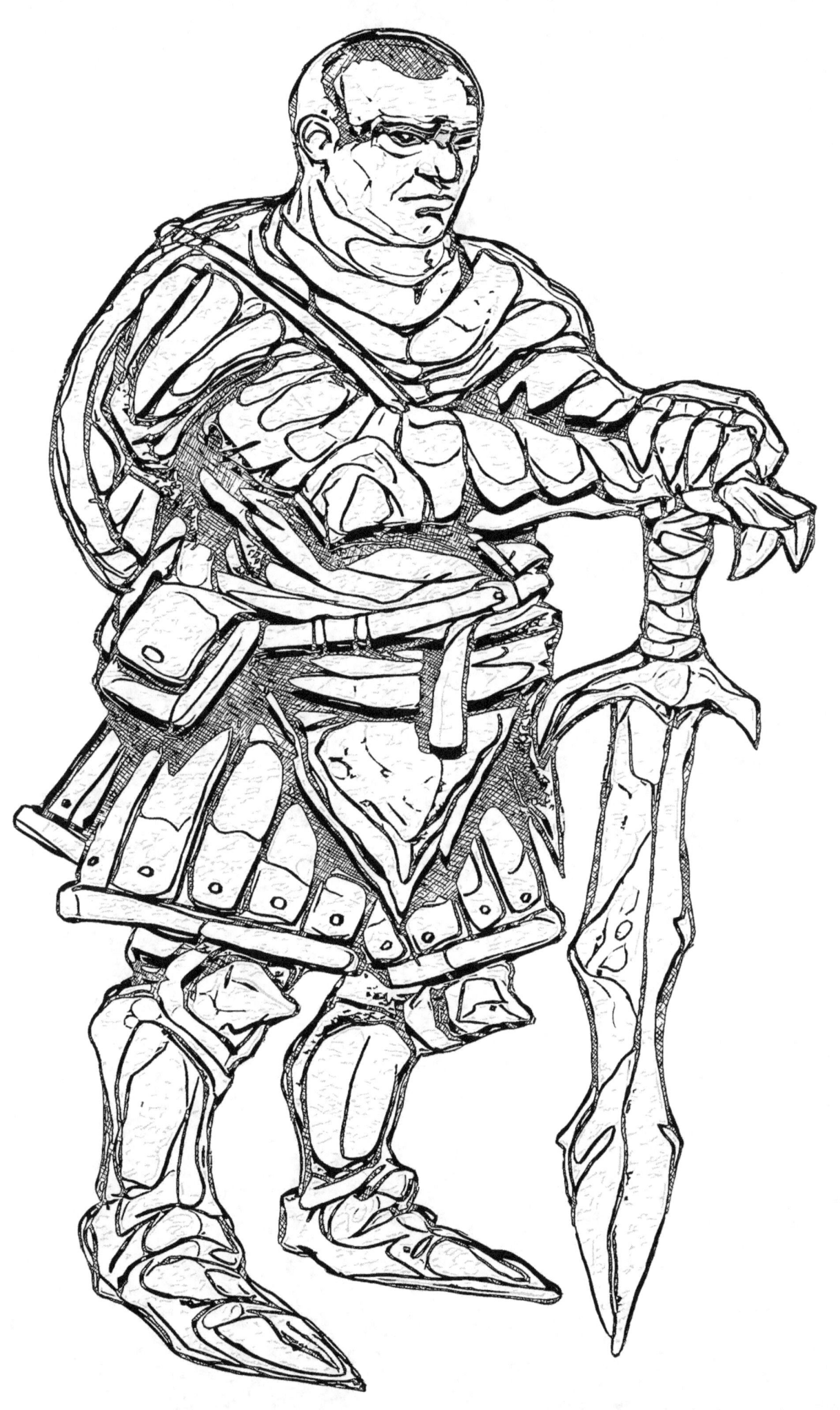

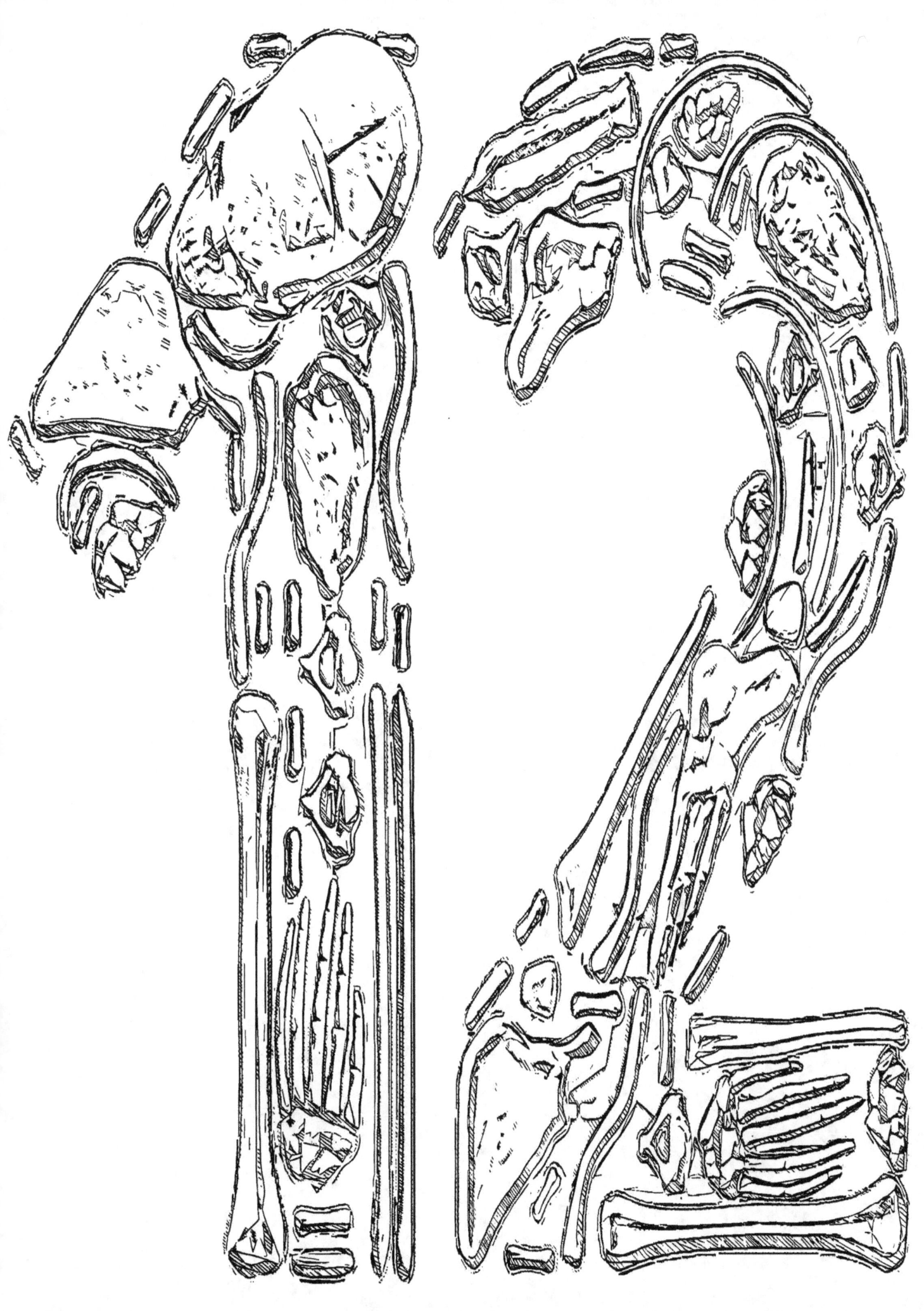

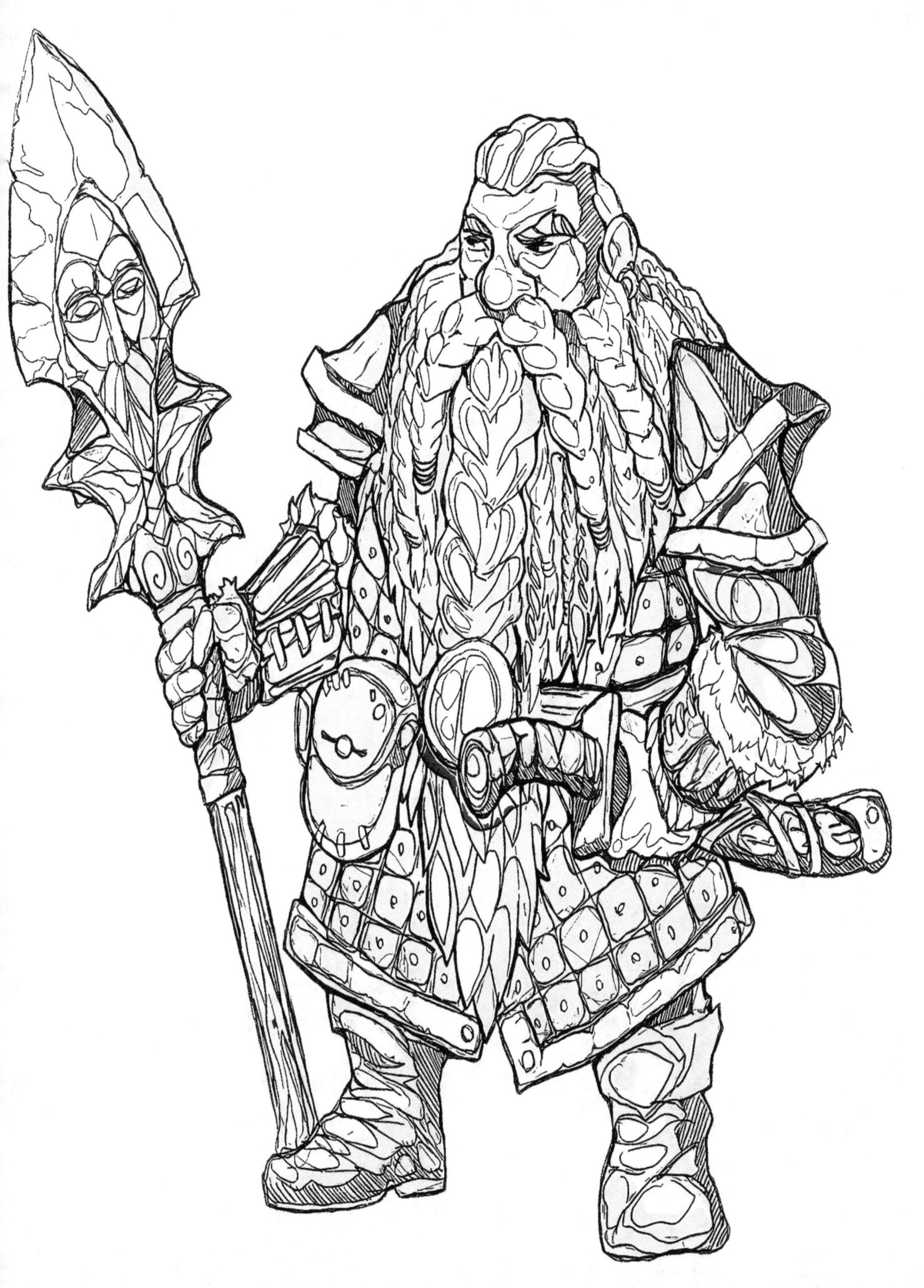

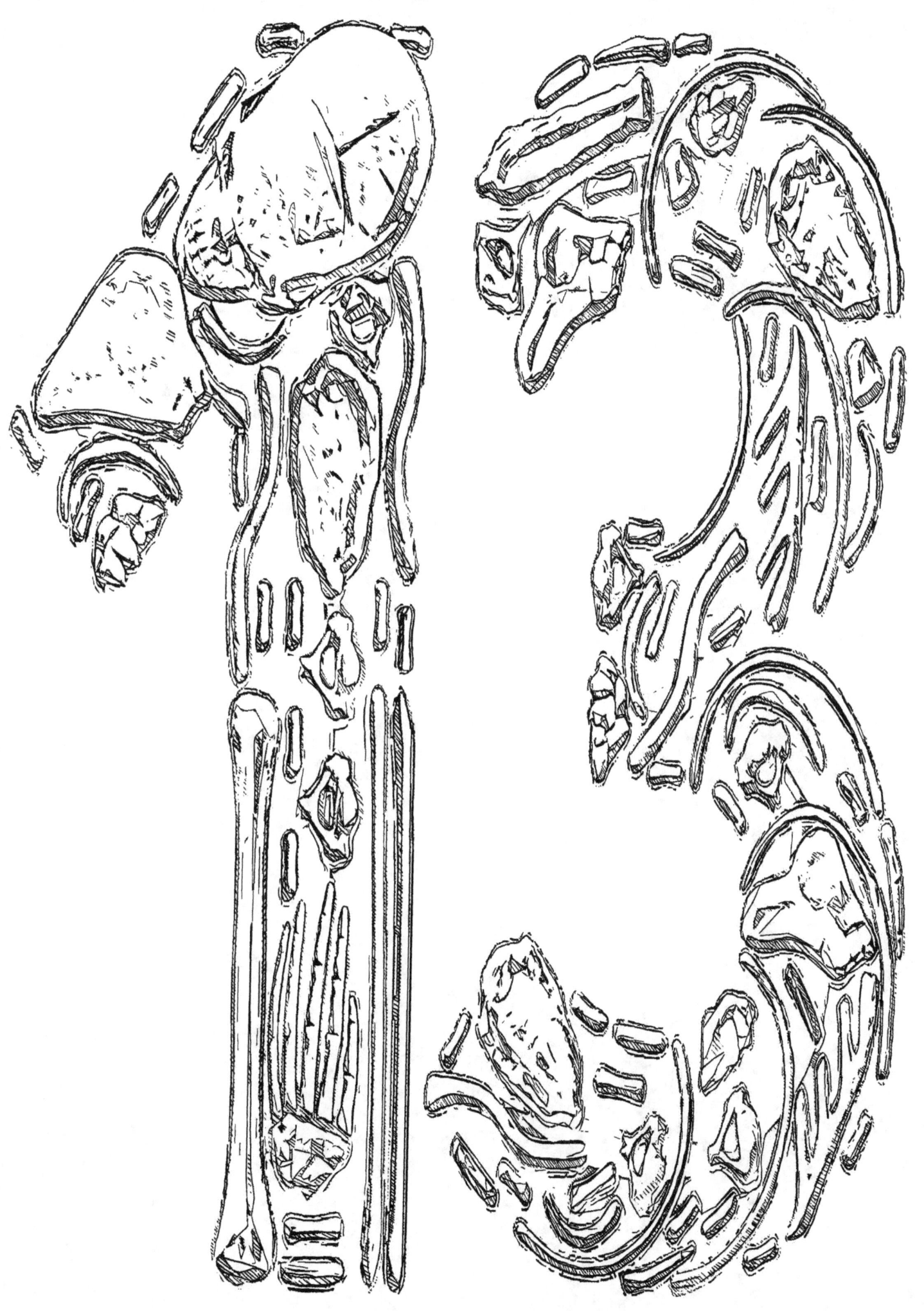

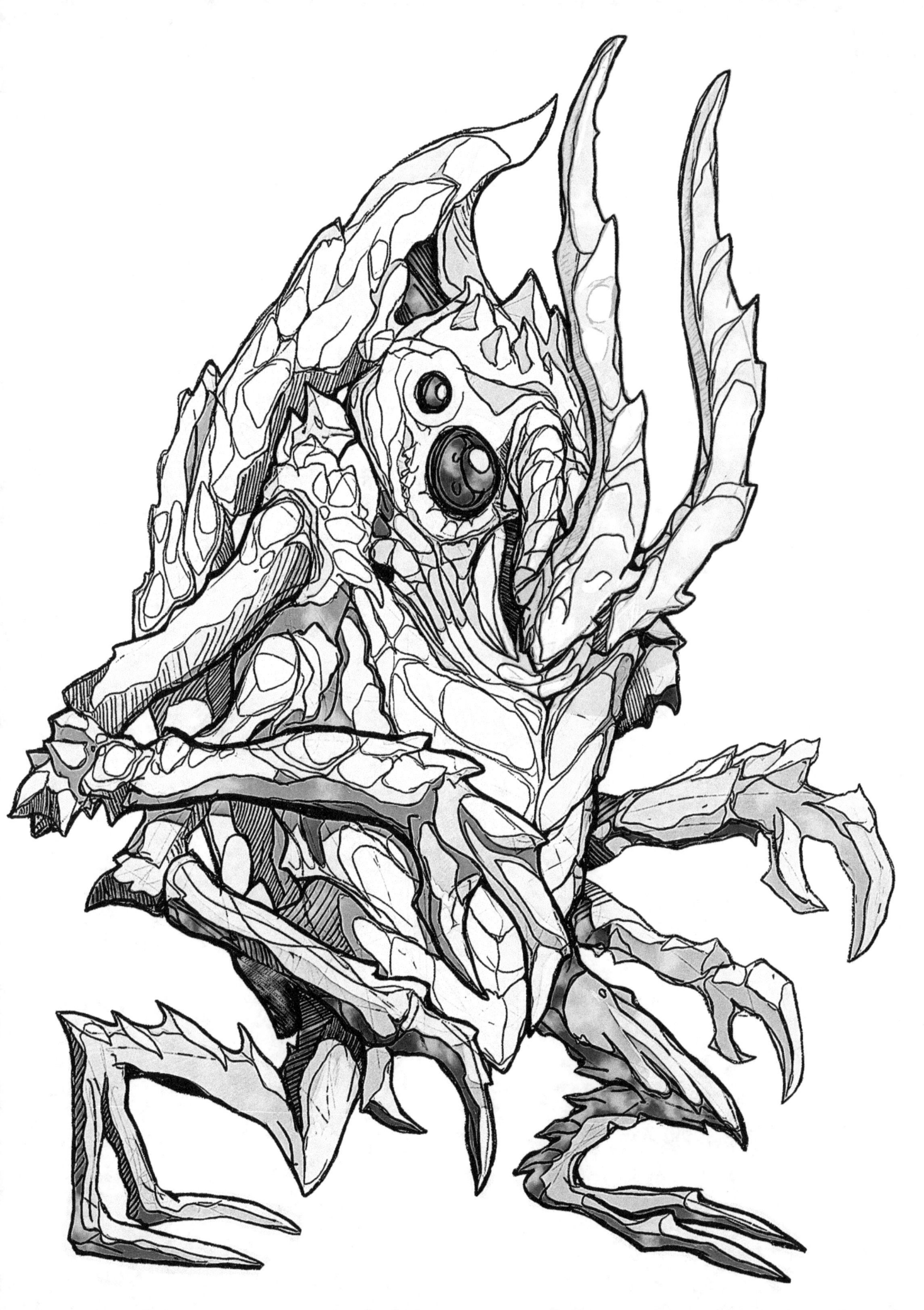

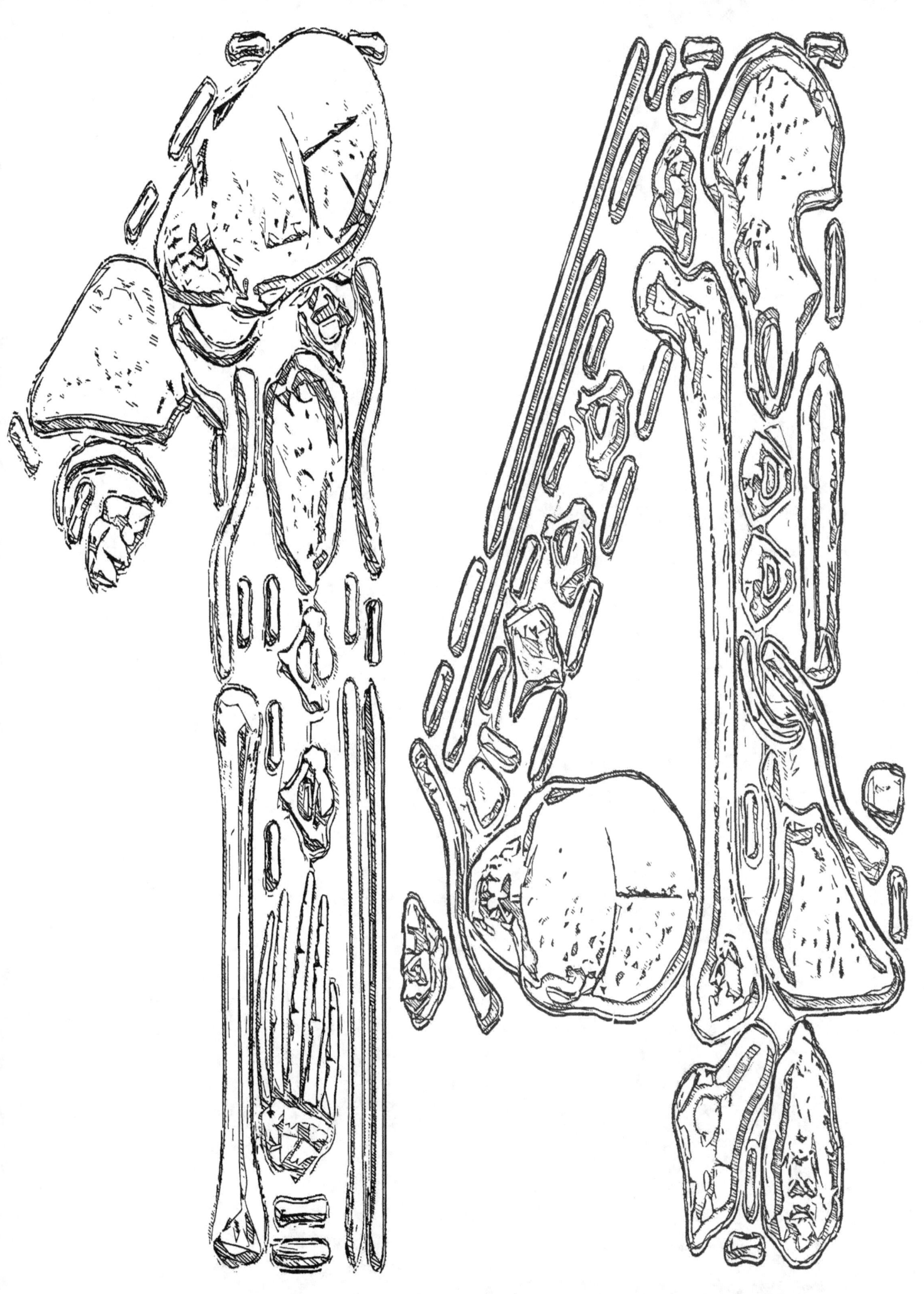

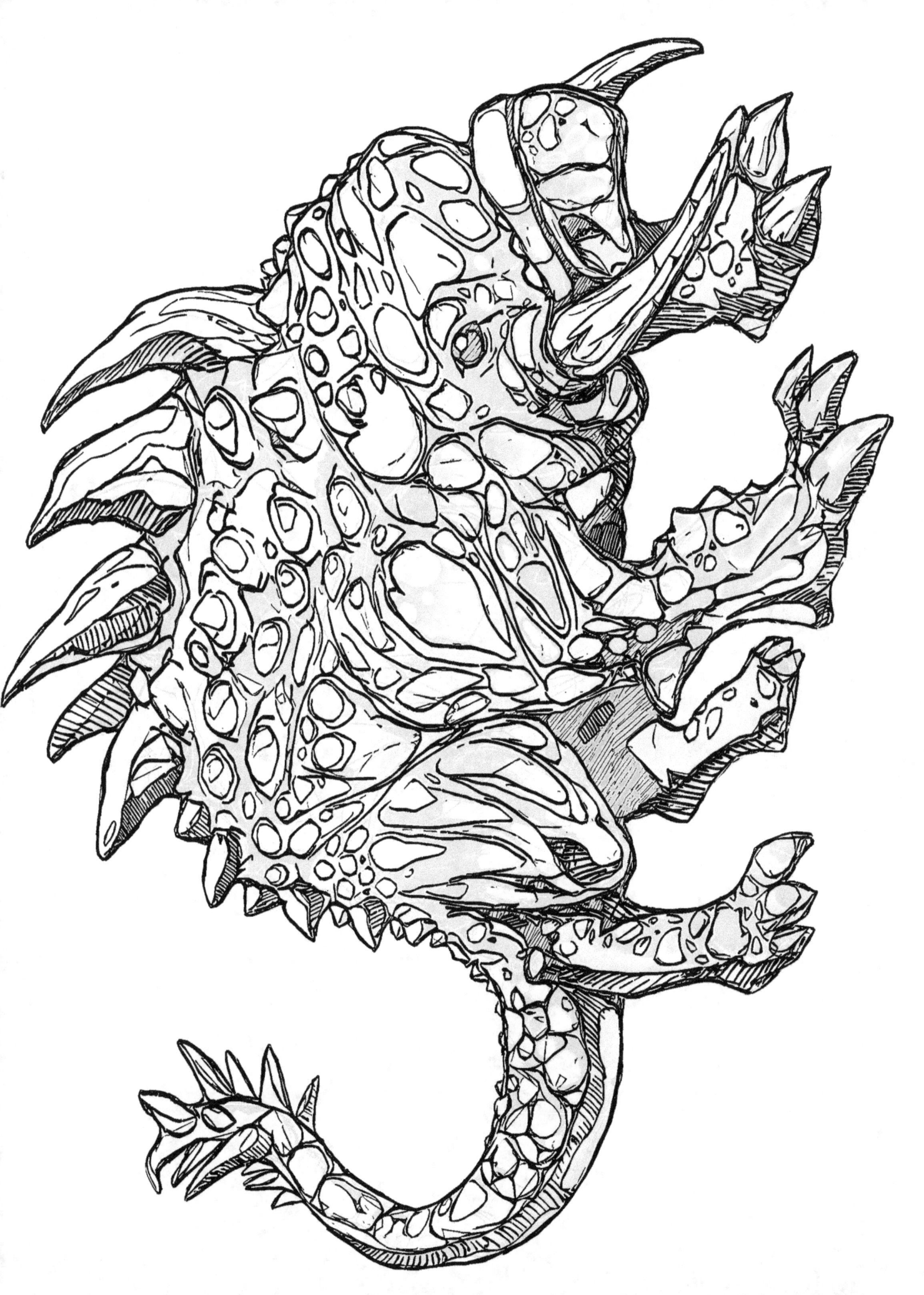

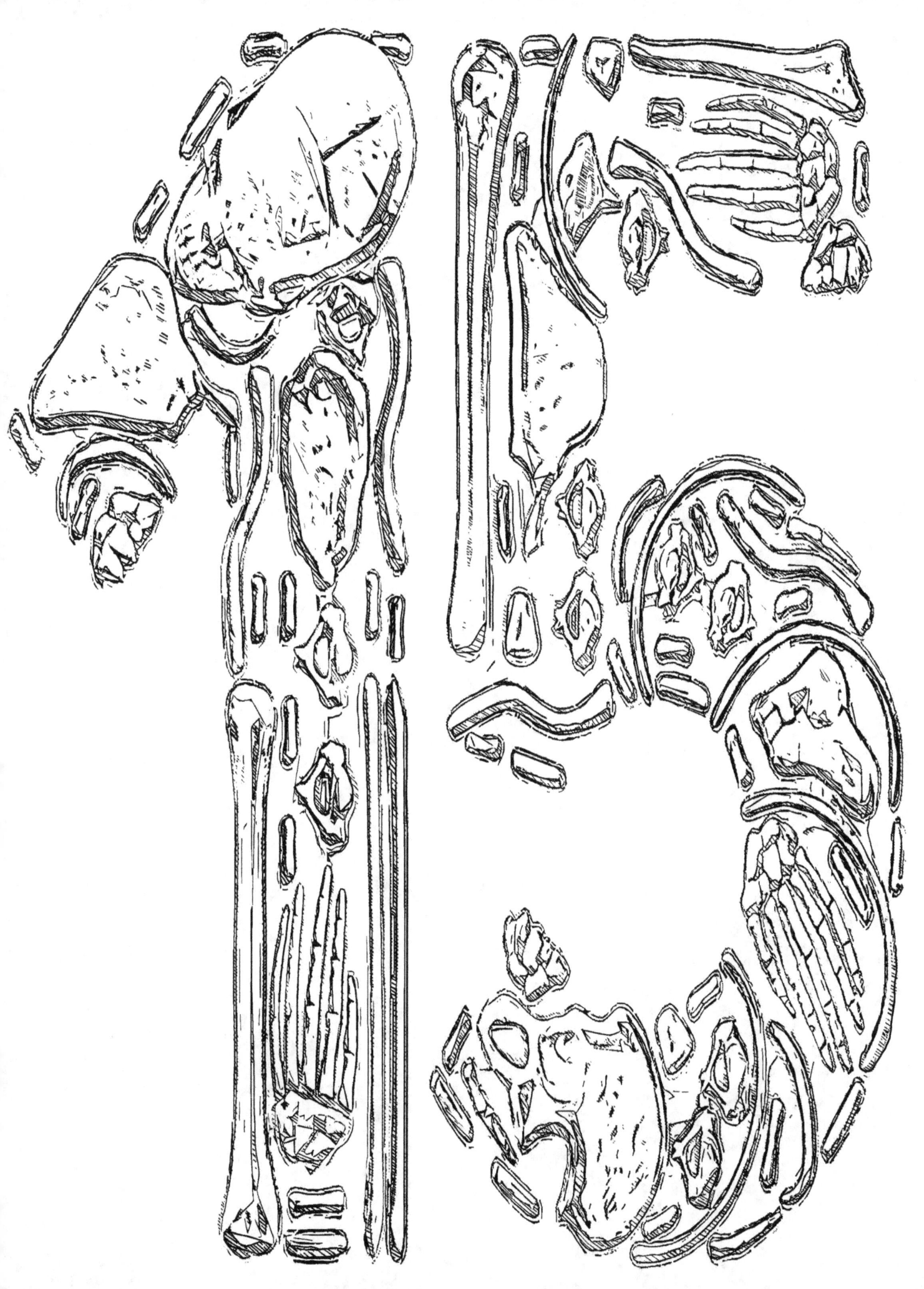

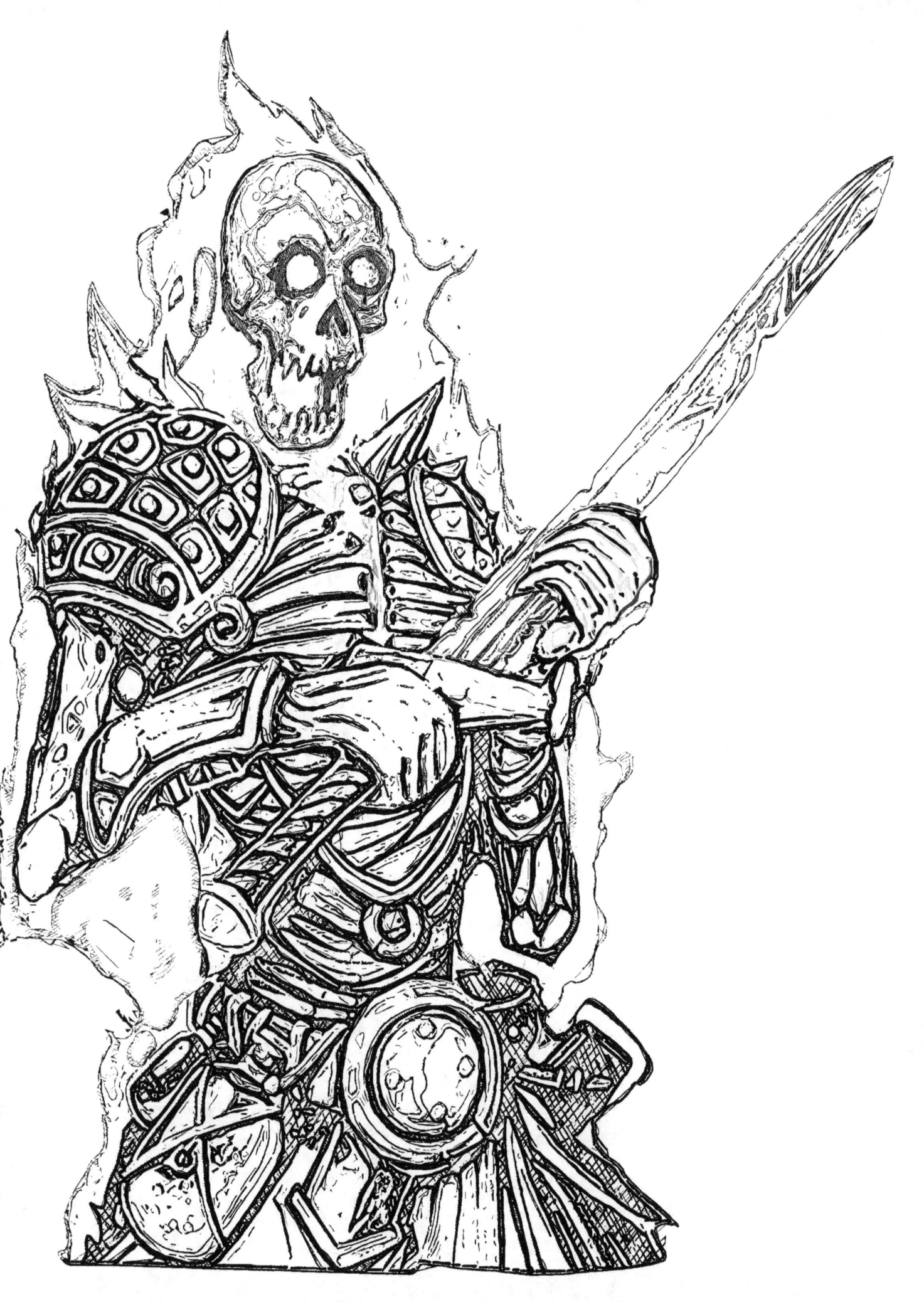

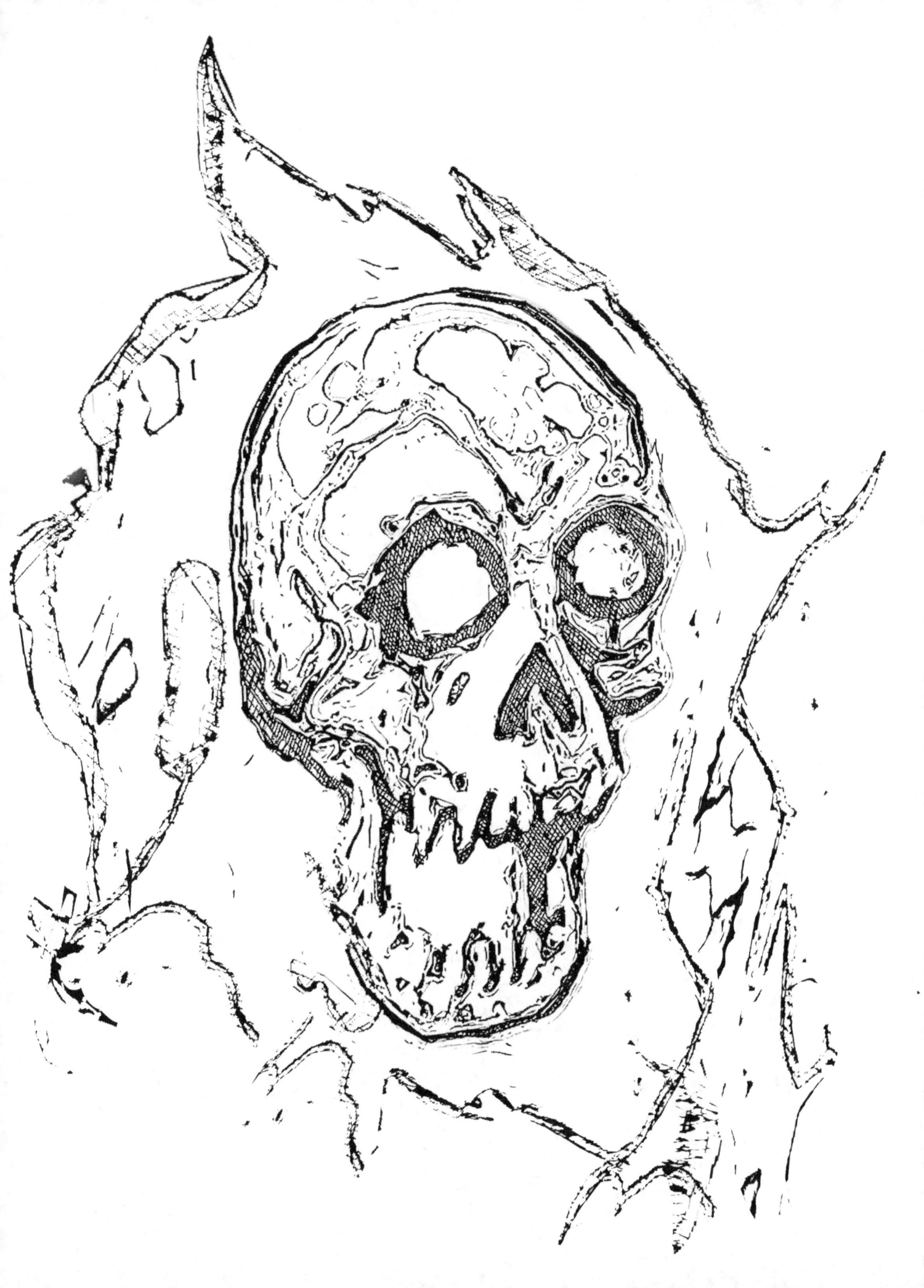

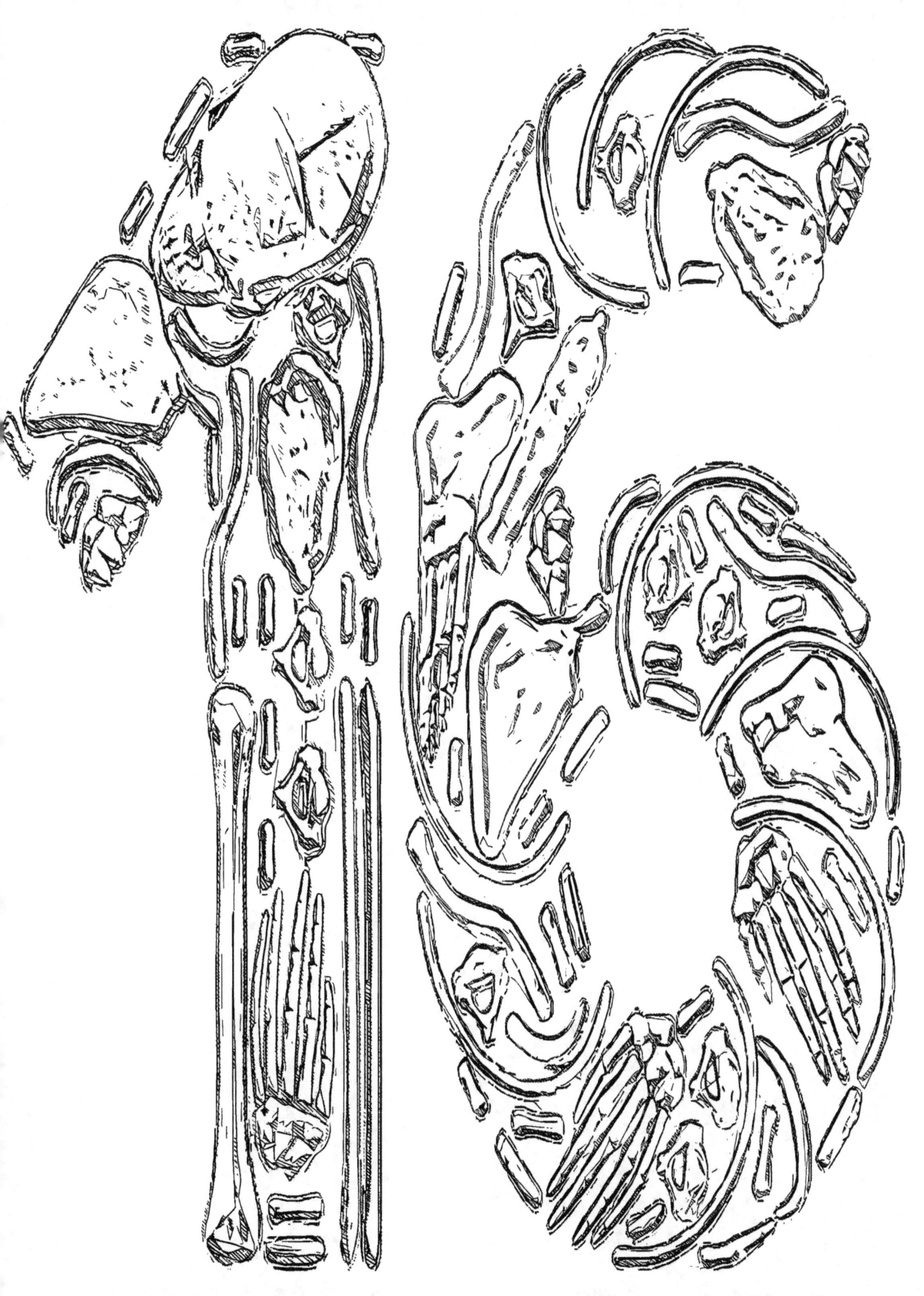

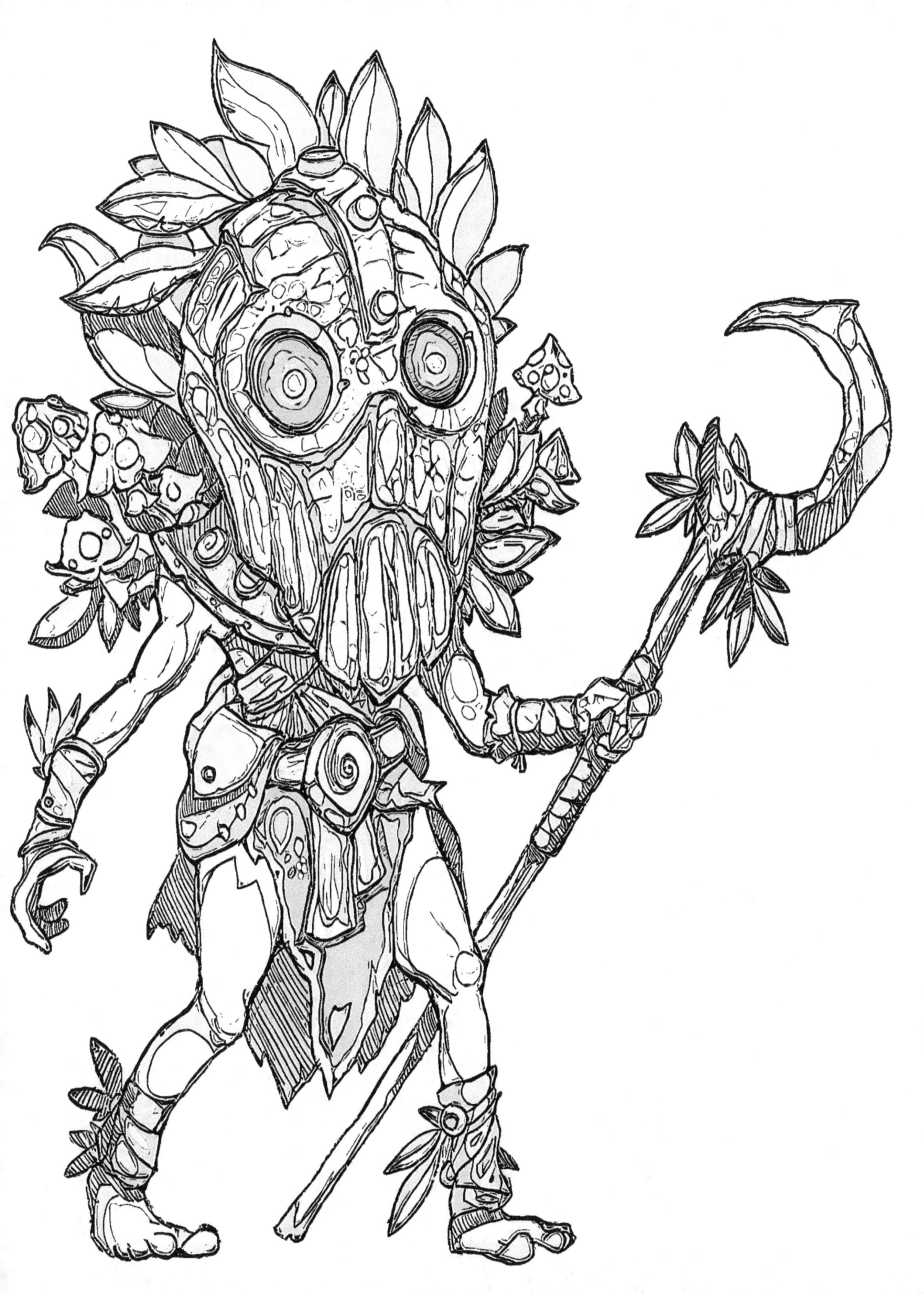

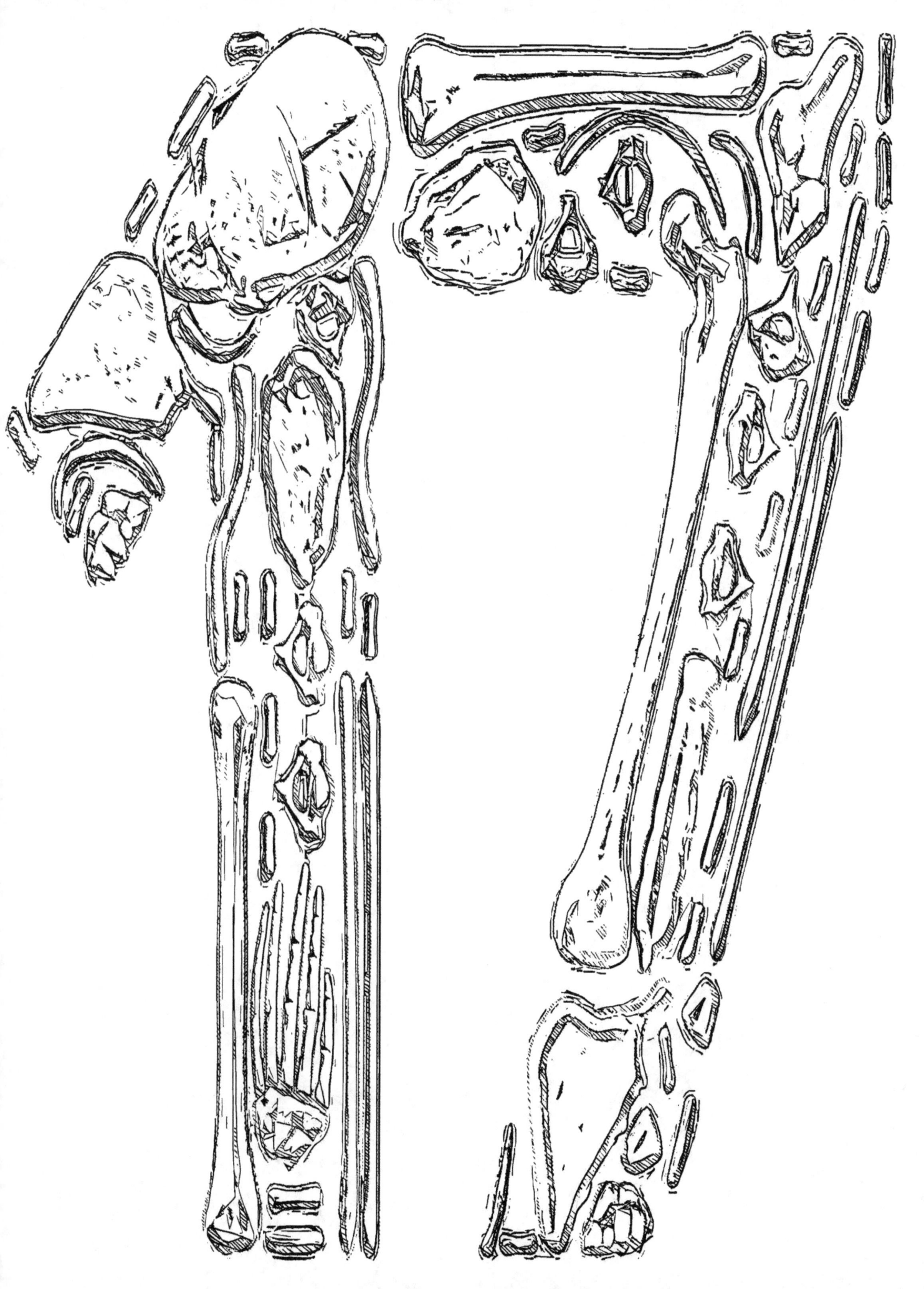

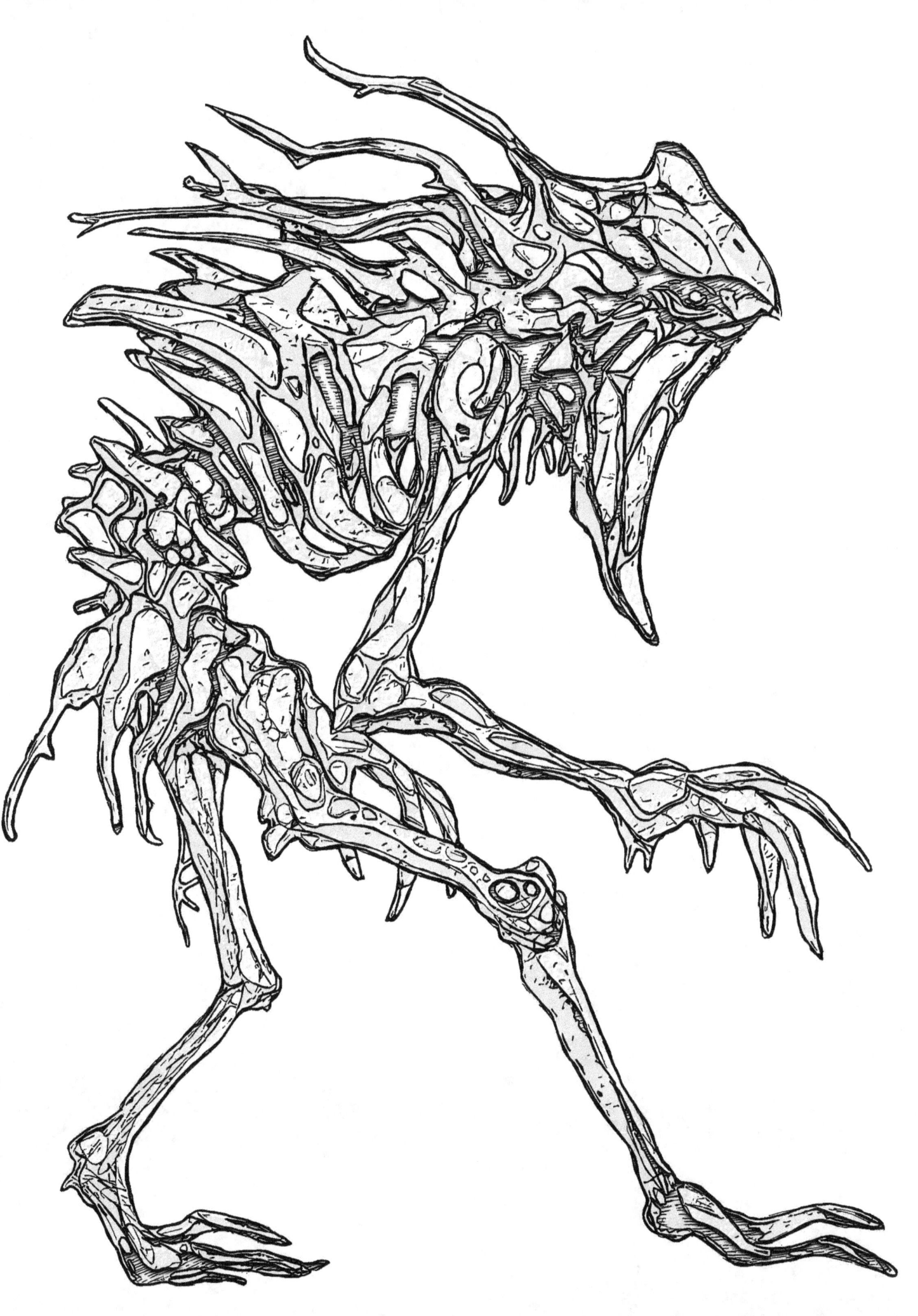

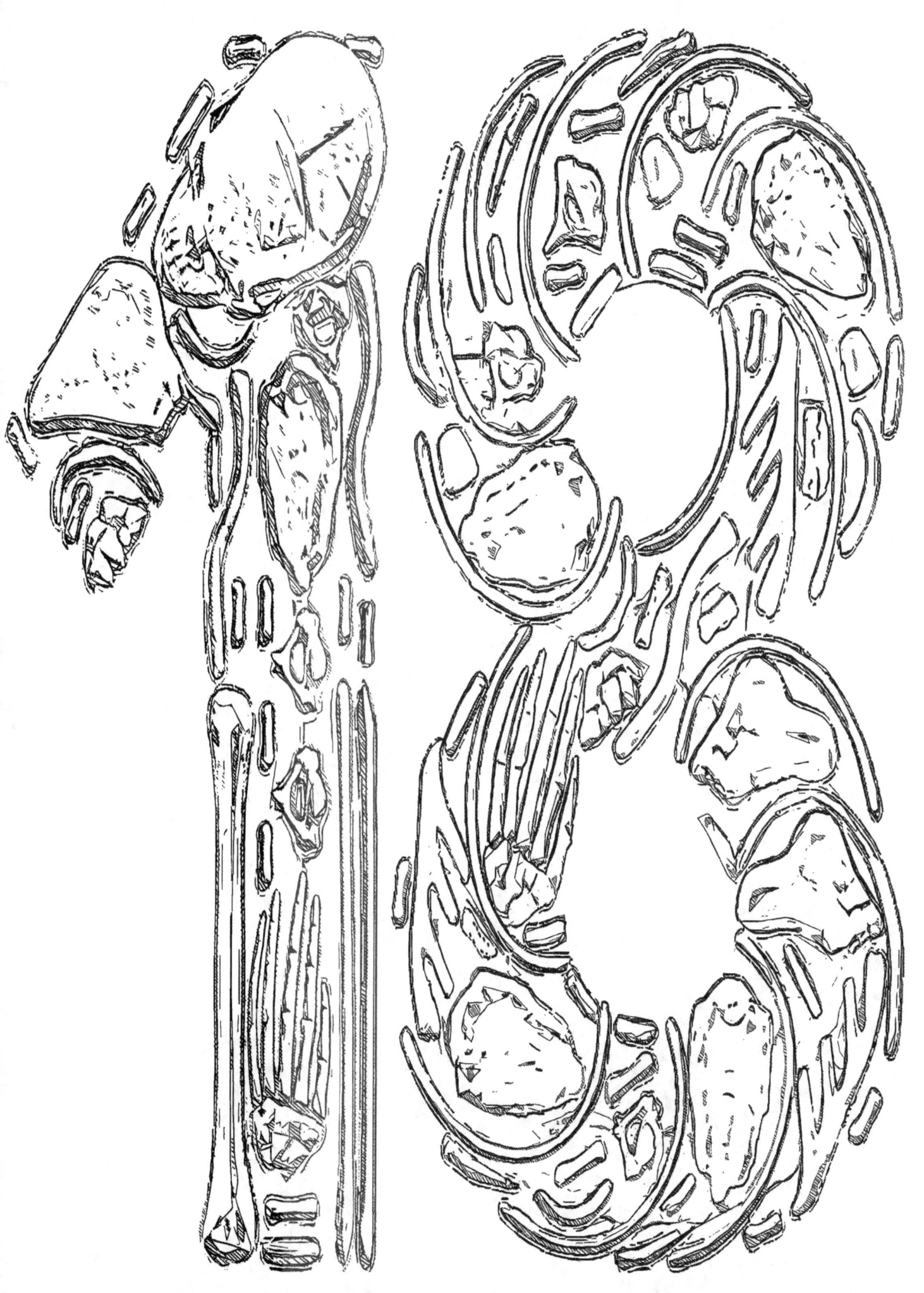

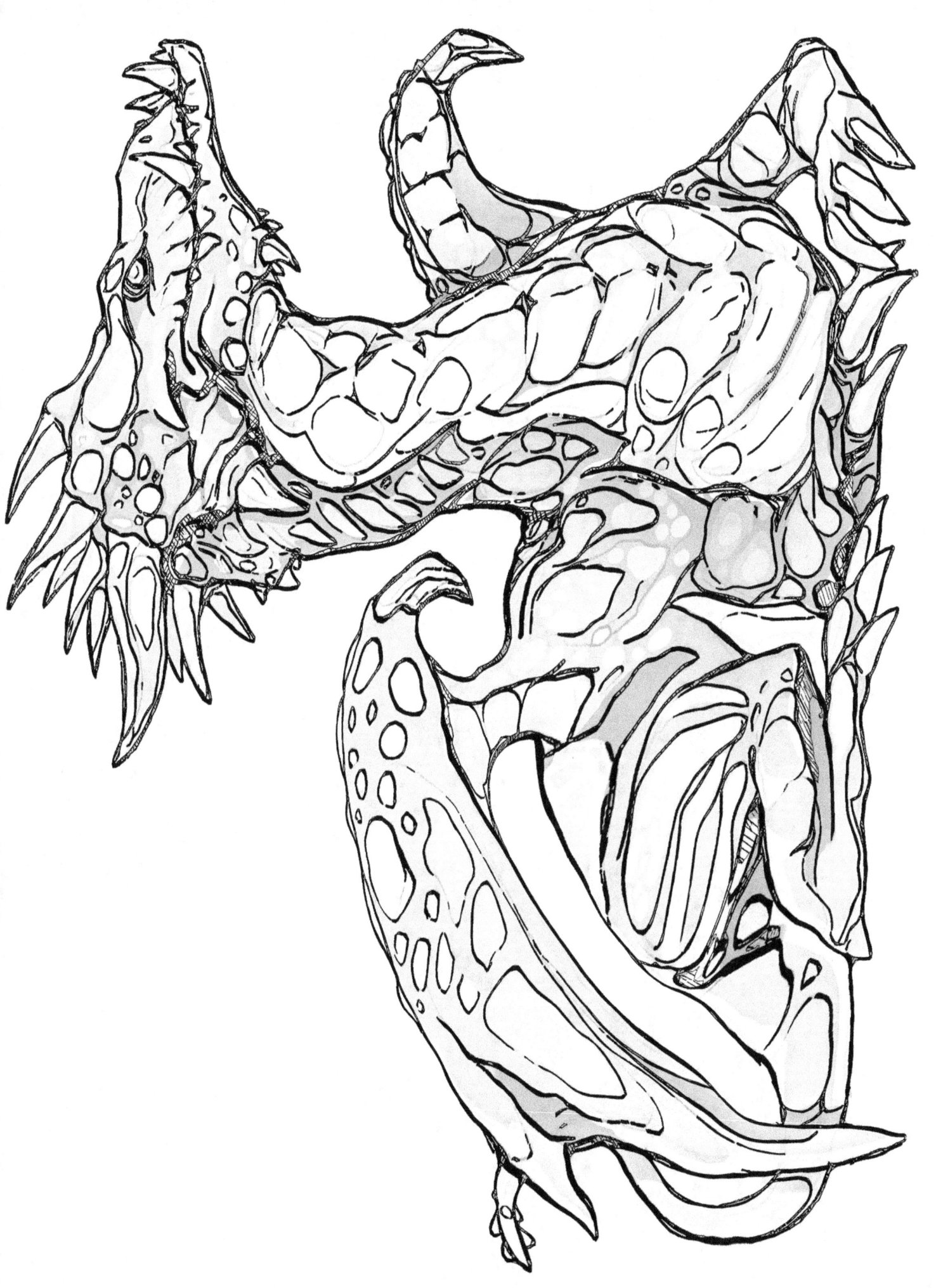

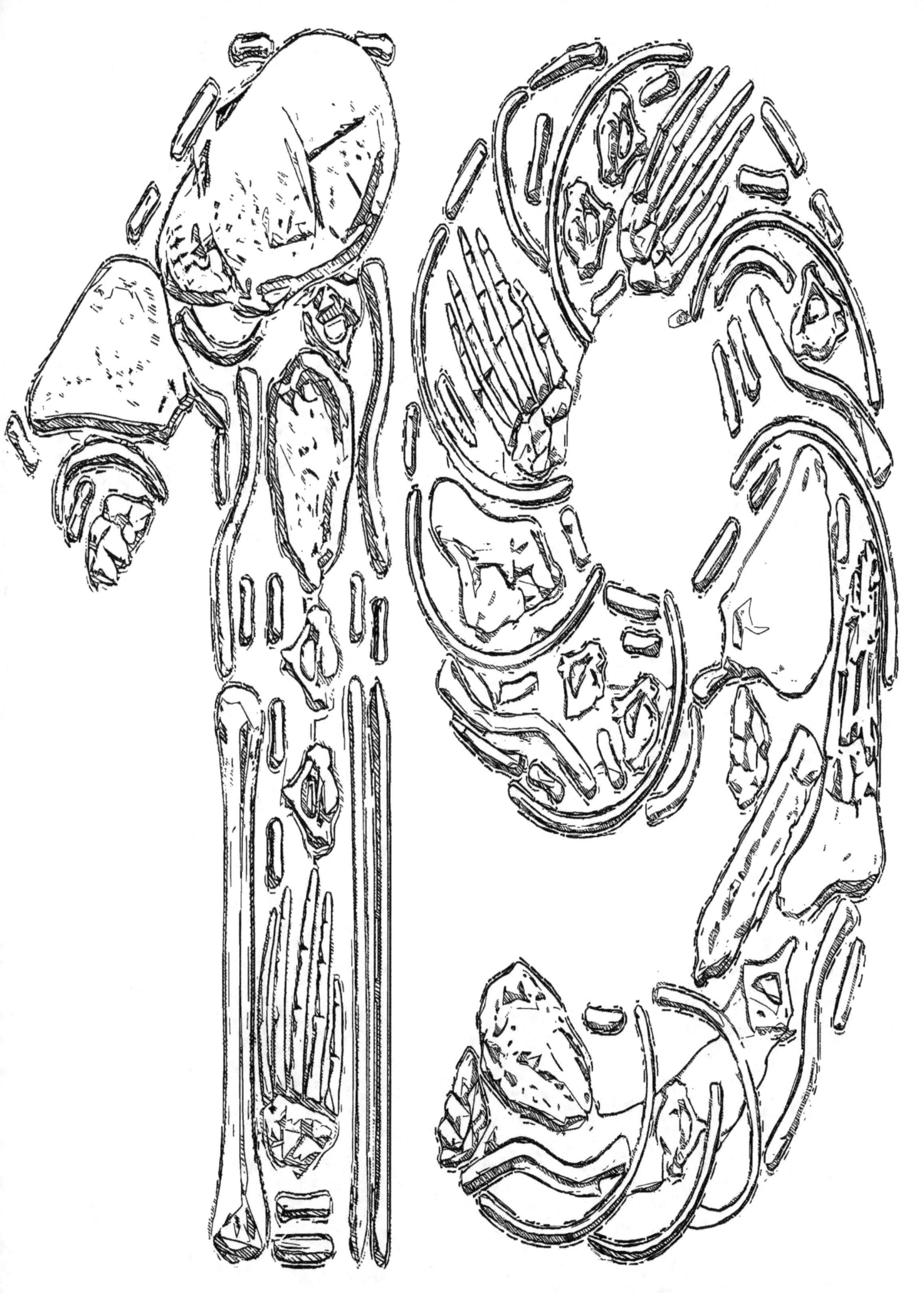

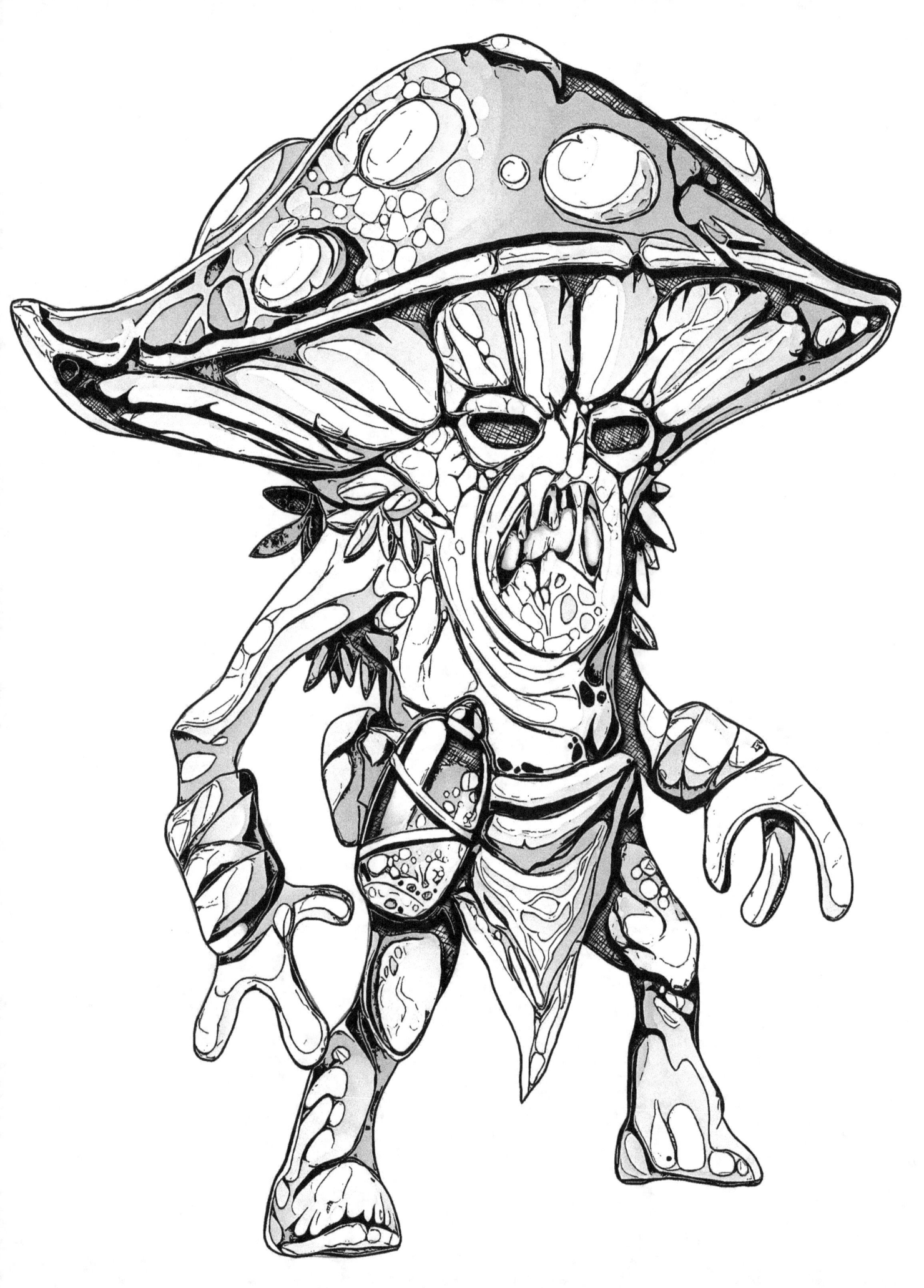

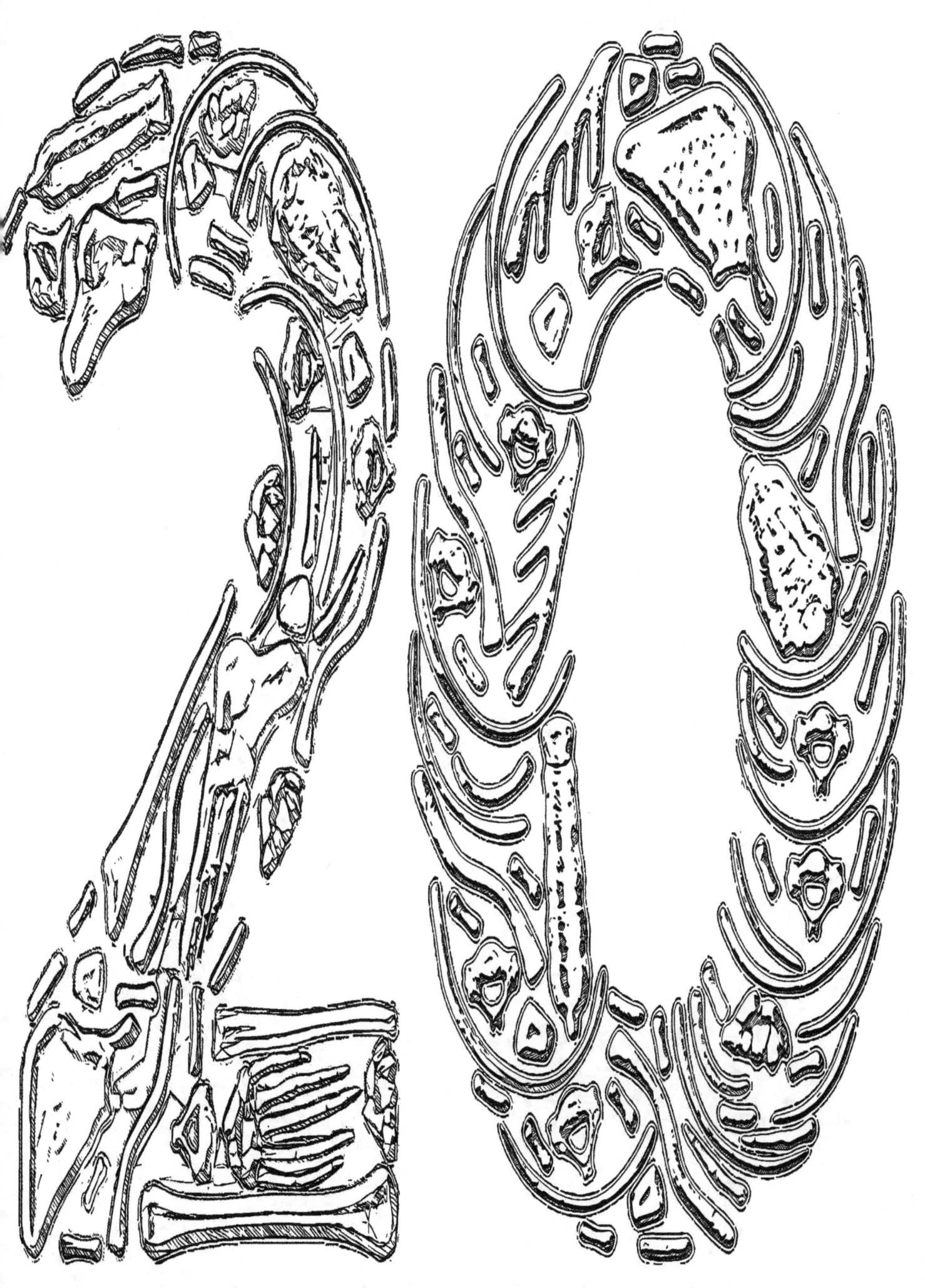

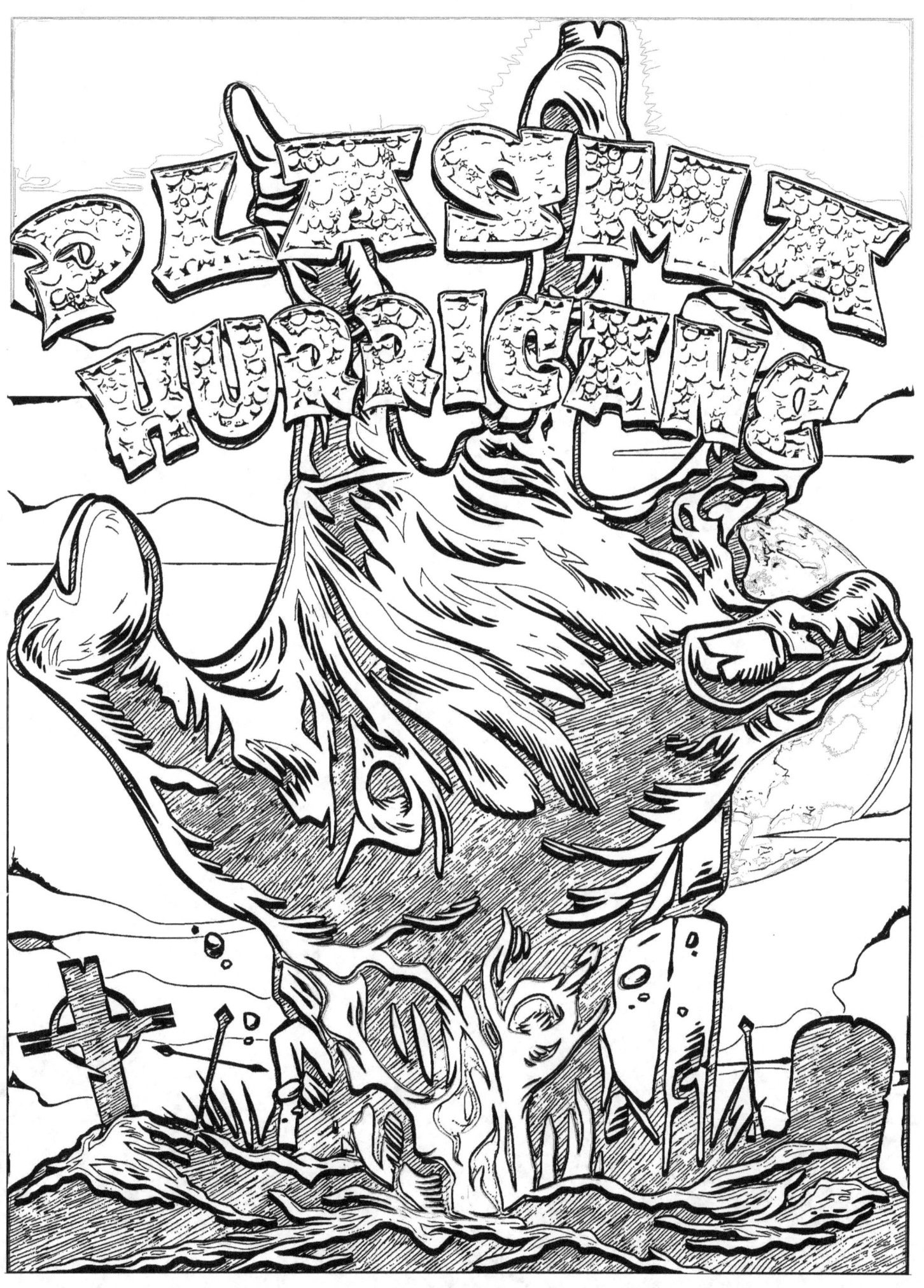

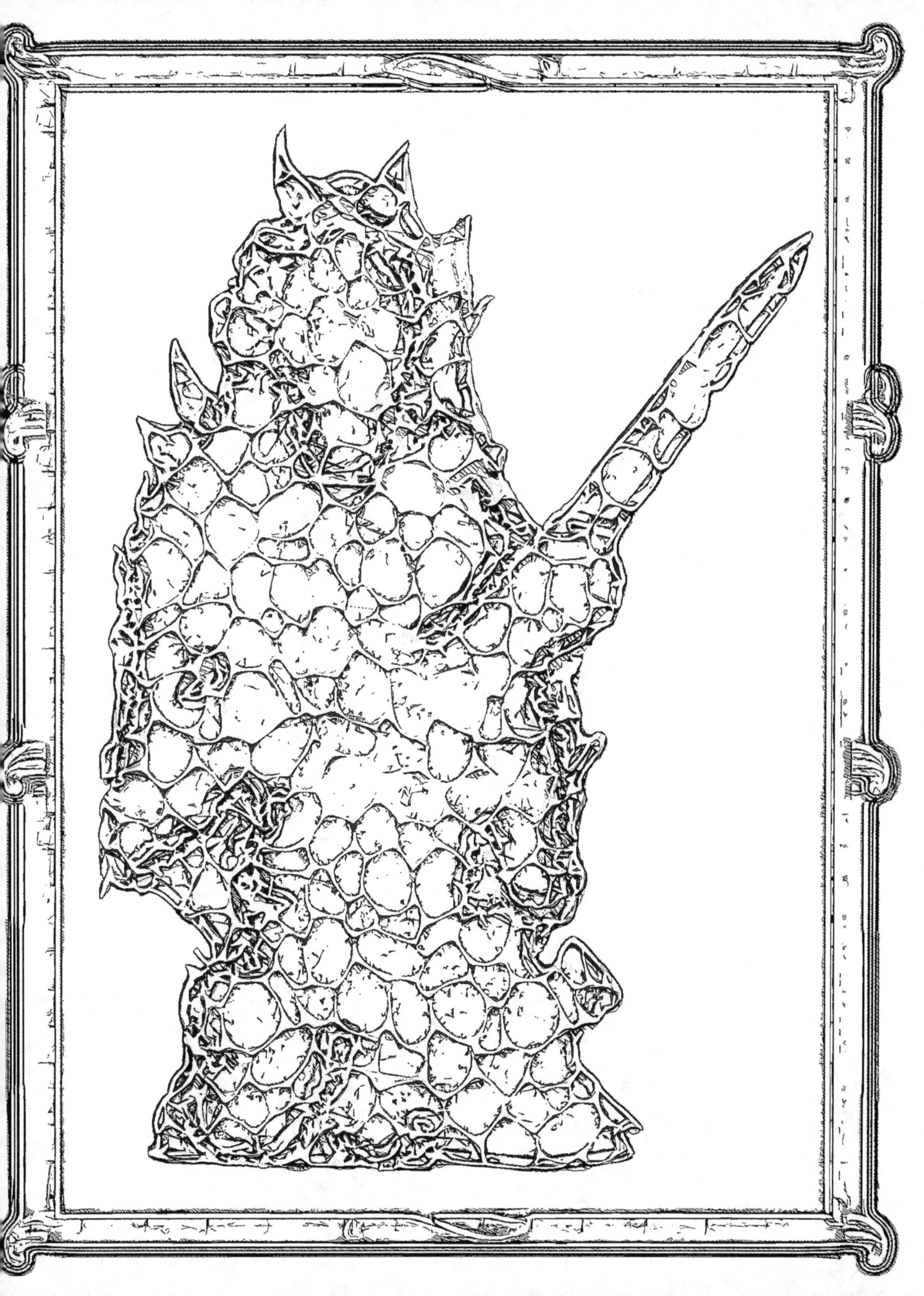

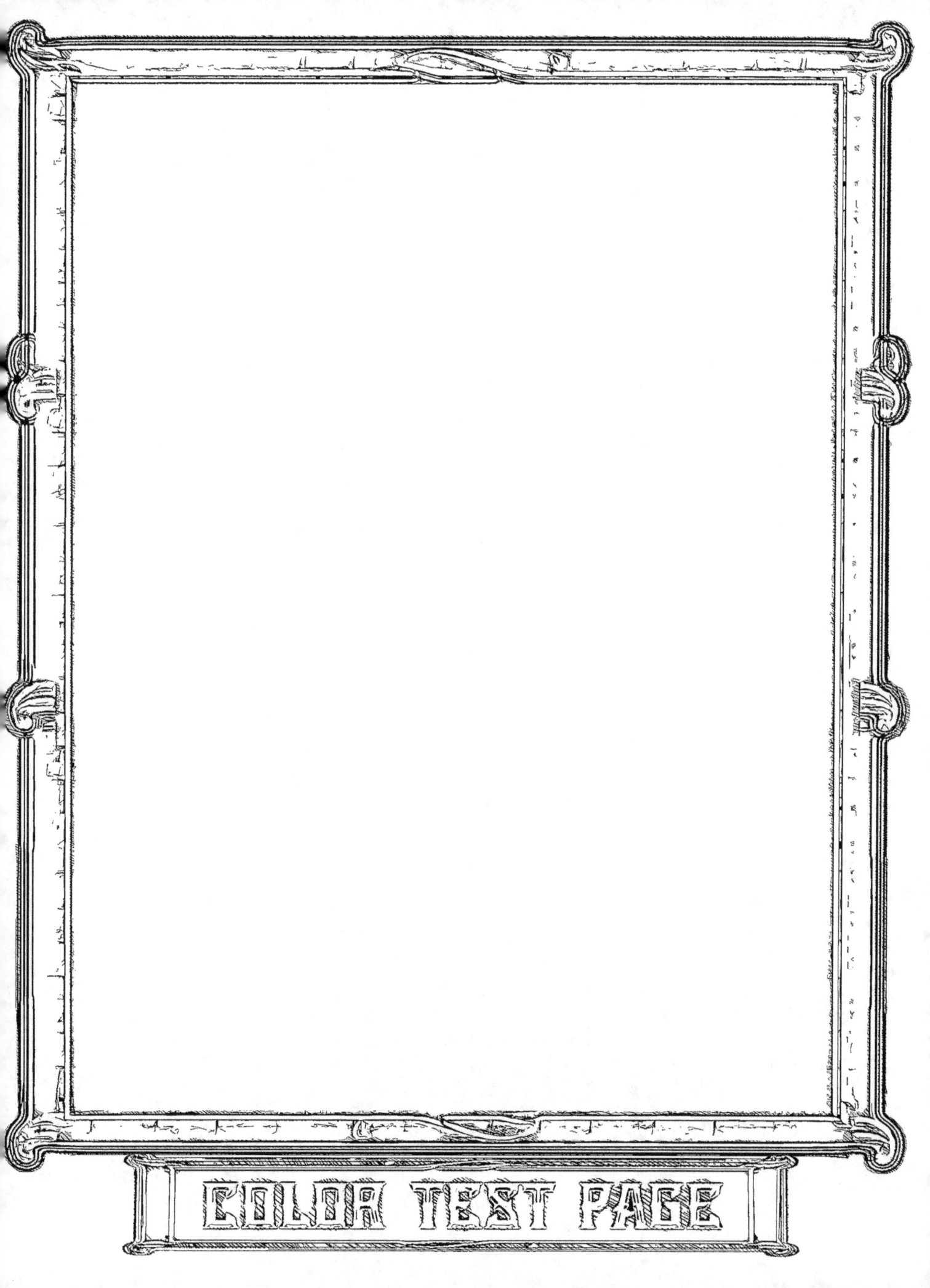

COLOR TEST PAGE

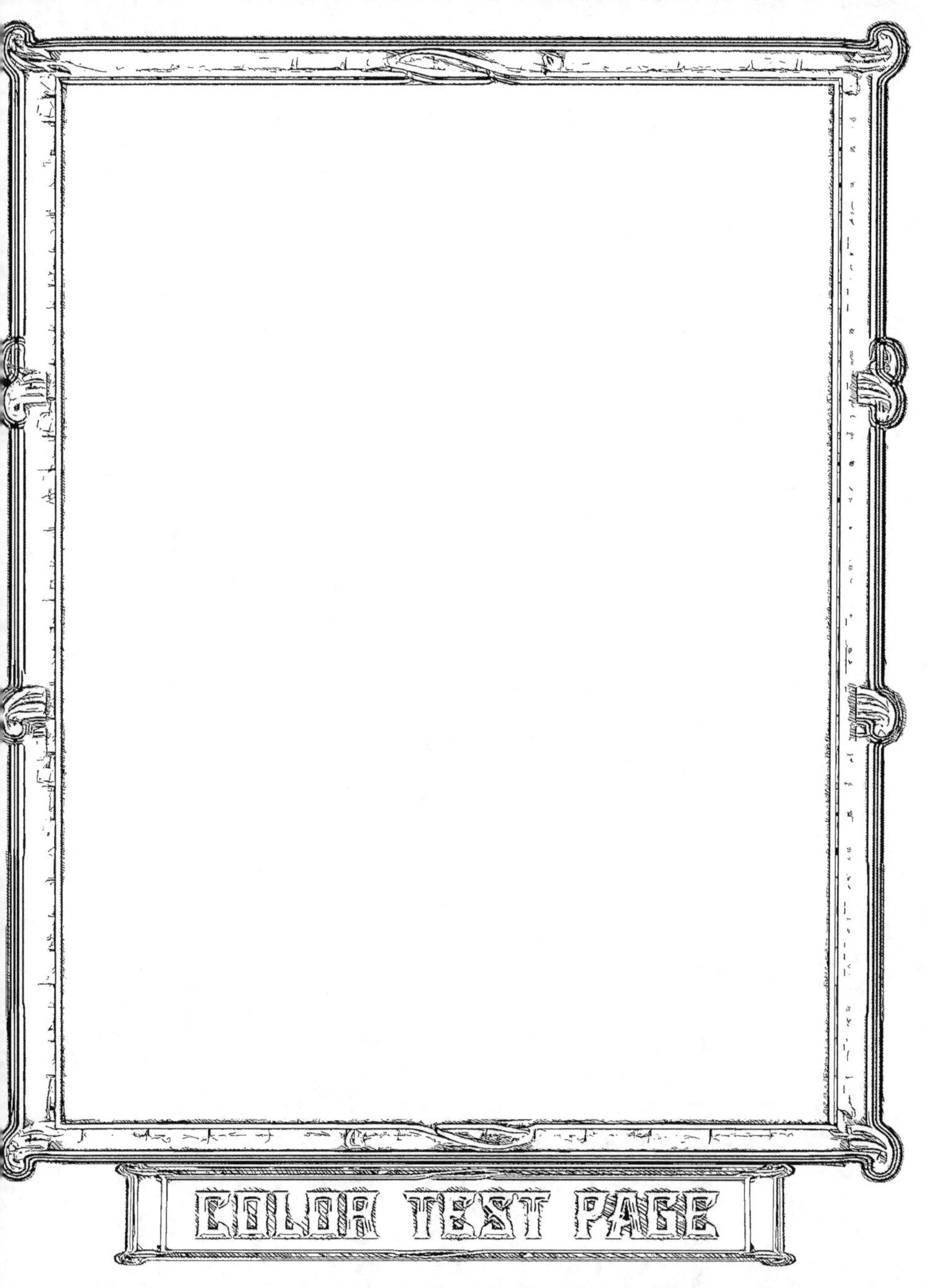

COLOR TEST PAGE

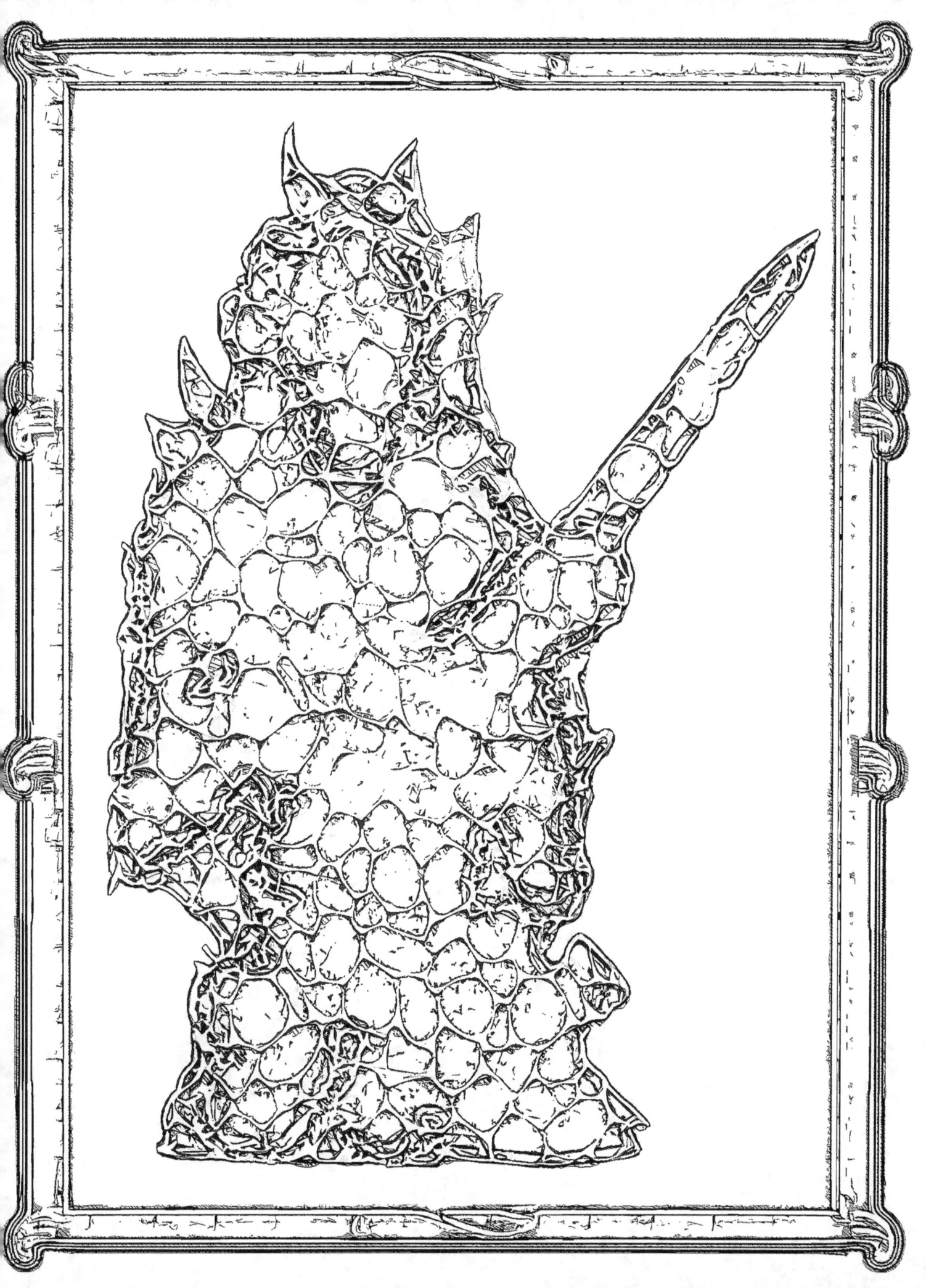

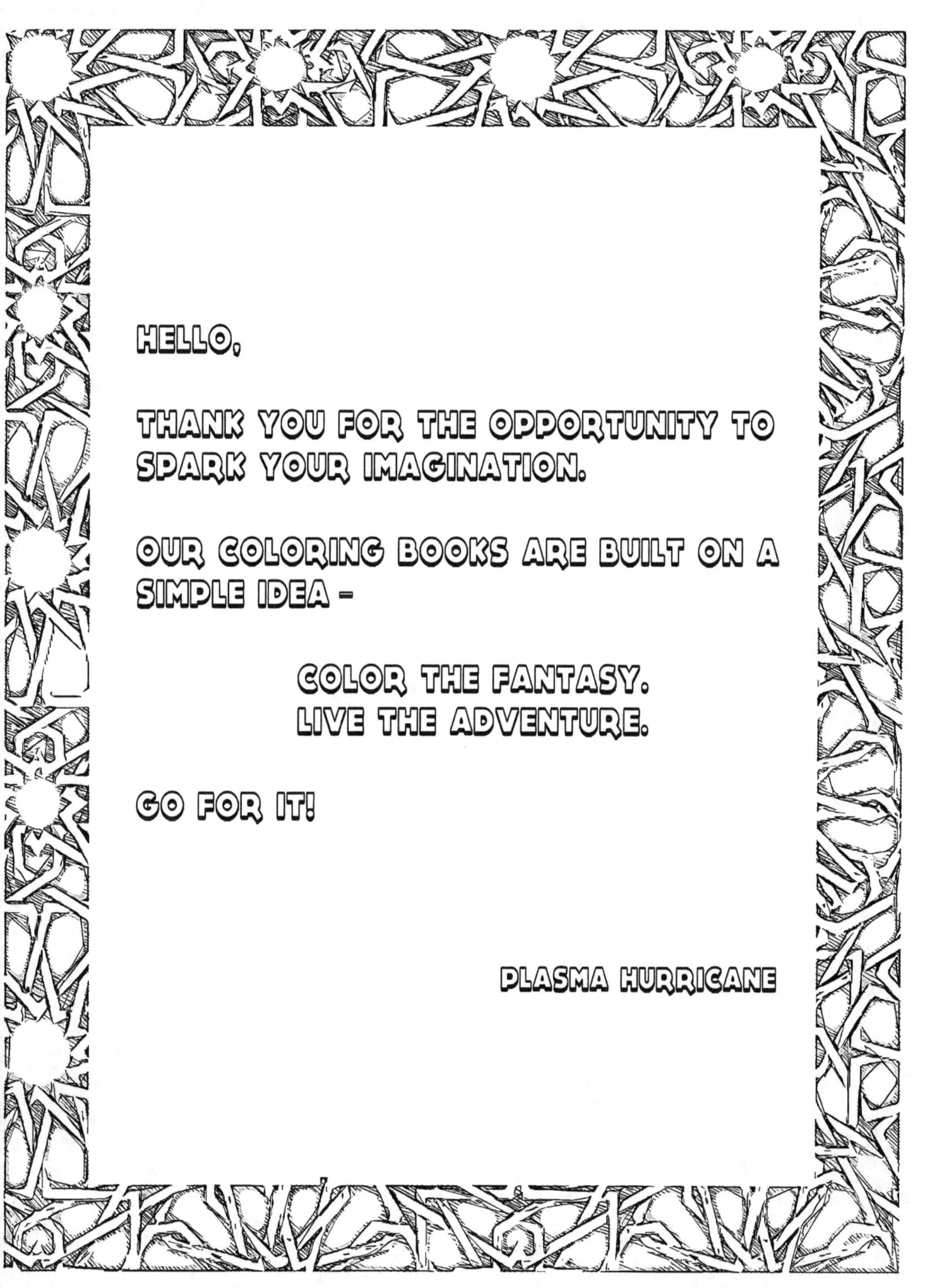

HELLO,

THANK YOU FOR THE OPPORTUNITY TO
SPARK YOUR IMAGINATION.

OUR COLORING BOOKS ARE BUILT ON A
SIMPLE IDEA -

COLOR THE FANTASY.
LIVE THE ADVENTURE.

GO FOR IT!

PLASMA HURRICANE

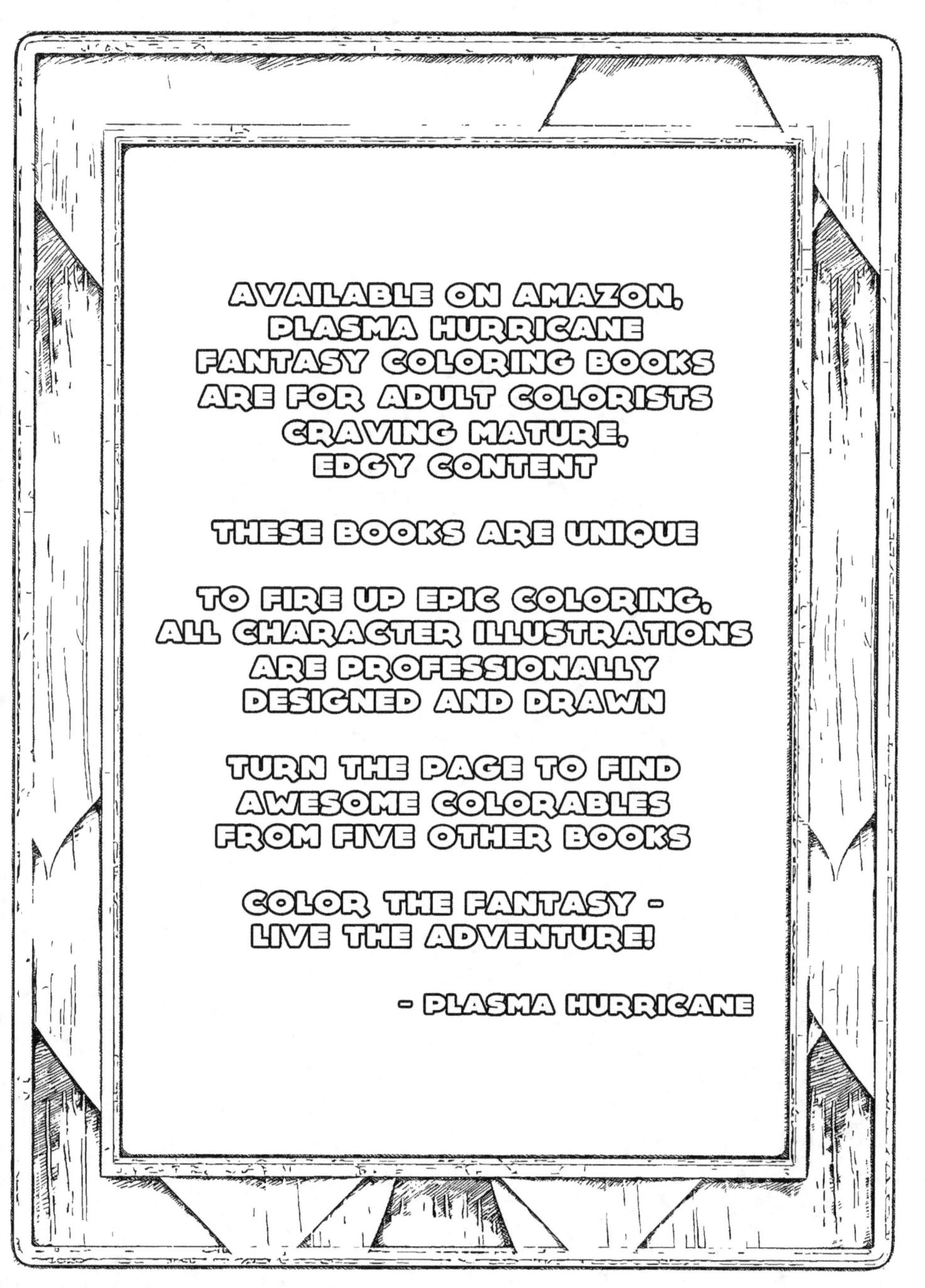

AVAILABLE ON AMAZON,
PLASMA HURRICANE
FANTASY COLORING BOOKS
ARE FOR ADULT COLORISTS
CRAVING MATURE,
EDGY CONTENT

THESE BOOKS ARE UNIQUE

TO FIRE UP EPIC COLORING,
ALL CHARACTER ILLUSTRATIONS
ARE PROFESSIONALLY
DESIGNED AND DRAWN

TURN THE PAGE TO FIND
AWESOME COLORABLES
FROM FIVE OTHER BOOKS

COLOR THE FANTASY -
LIVE THE ADVENTURE!

- PLASMA HURRICANE

>> 

EPIC

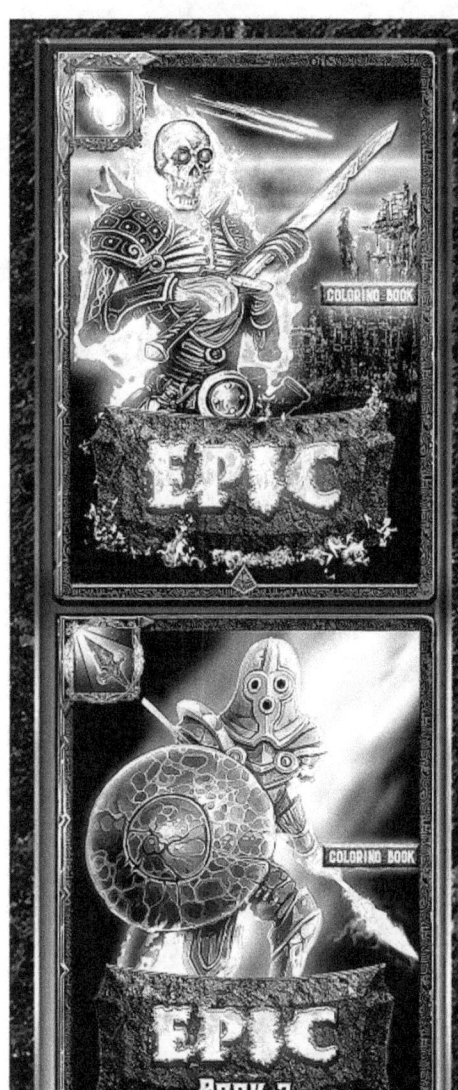

<< 

EPIC:
BOOK 2

>> 

COMBINES TWO
BOOKS:

EPIC

EPIC:
BOOK 2

<< 

ADORABLE
FREAKS

>> 

ADORABLE
FREAKS:
MAD HOUSE

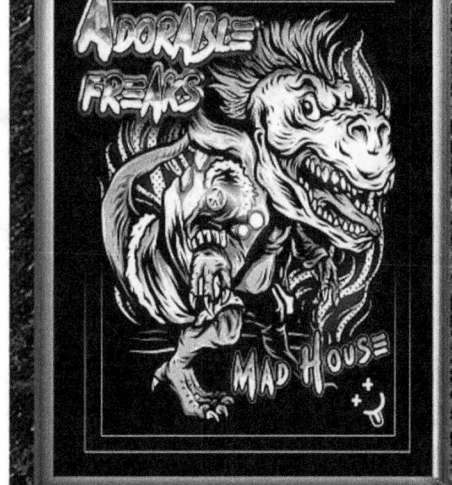

<< 

COMBINES TWO
BOOKS:

ADORABLE
FREAKS

ADORABLE
FREAKS:
MAD HOUSE

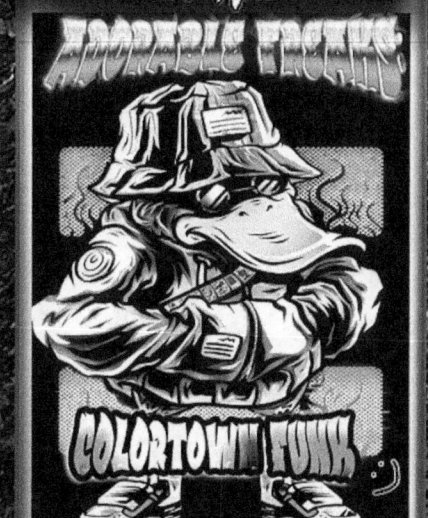

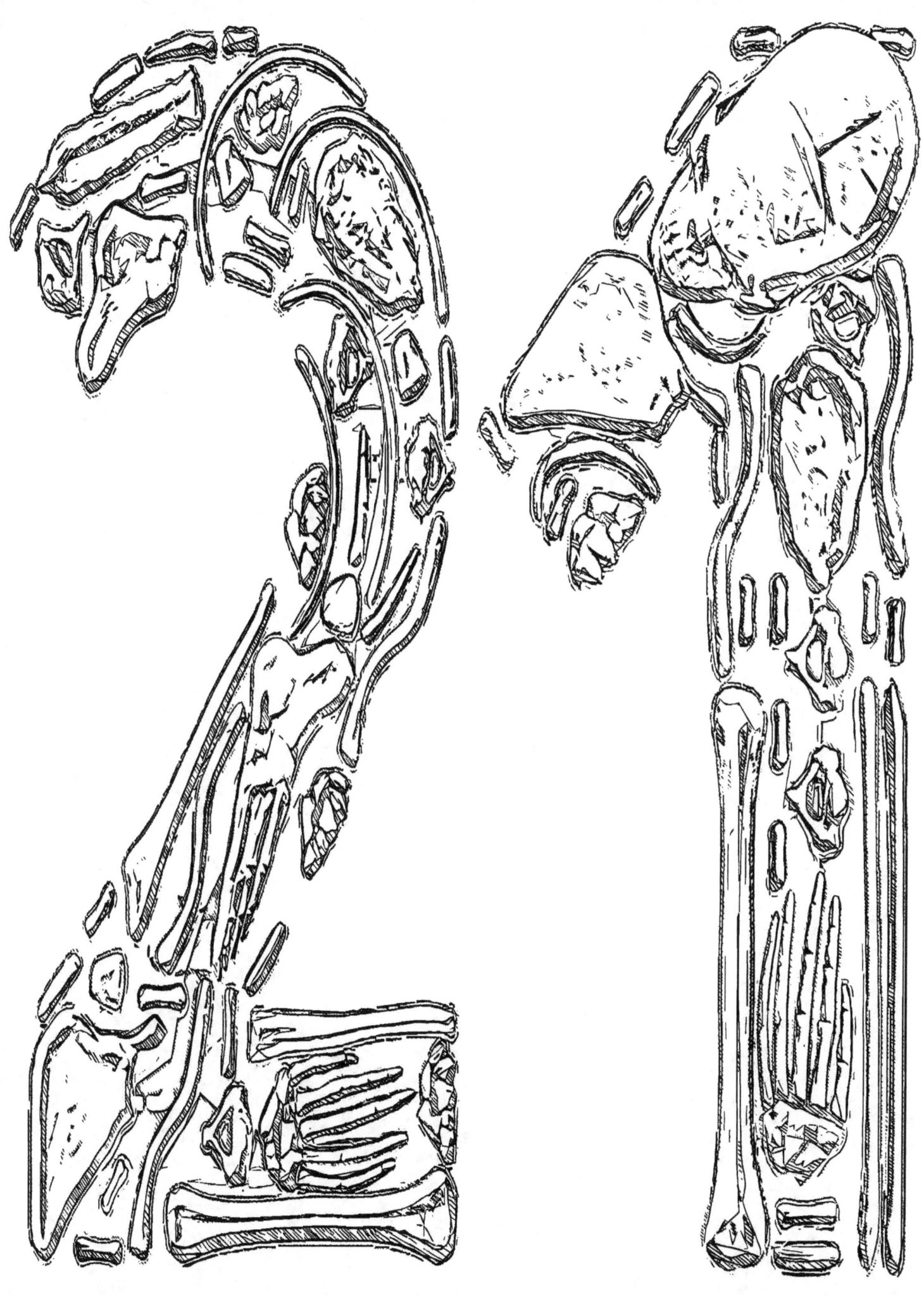

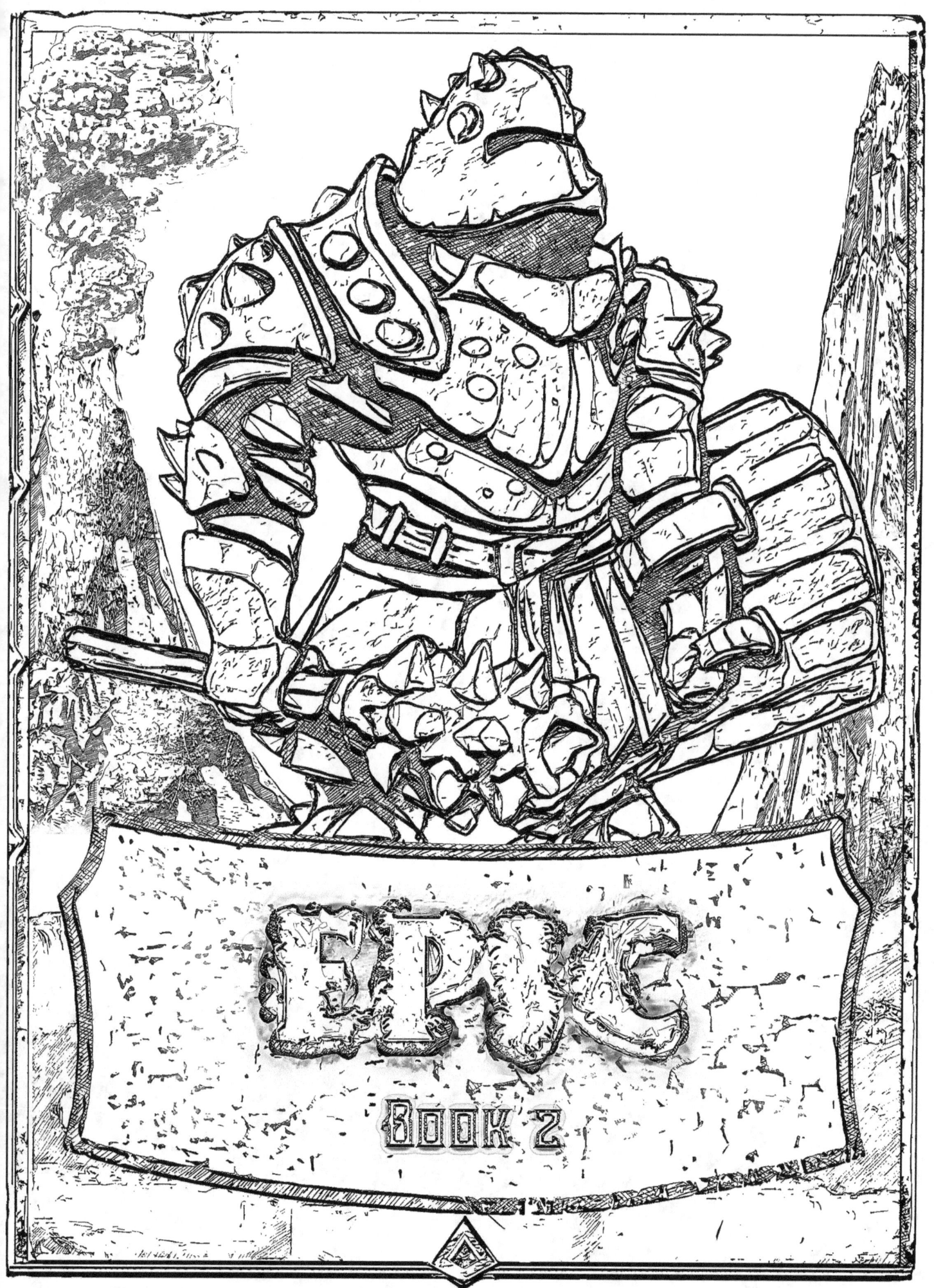

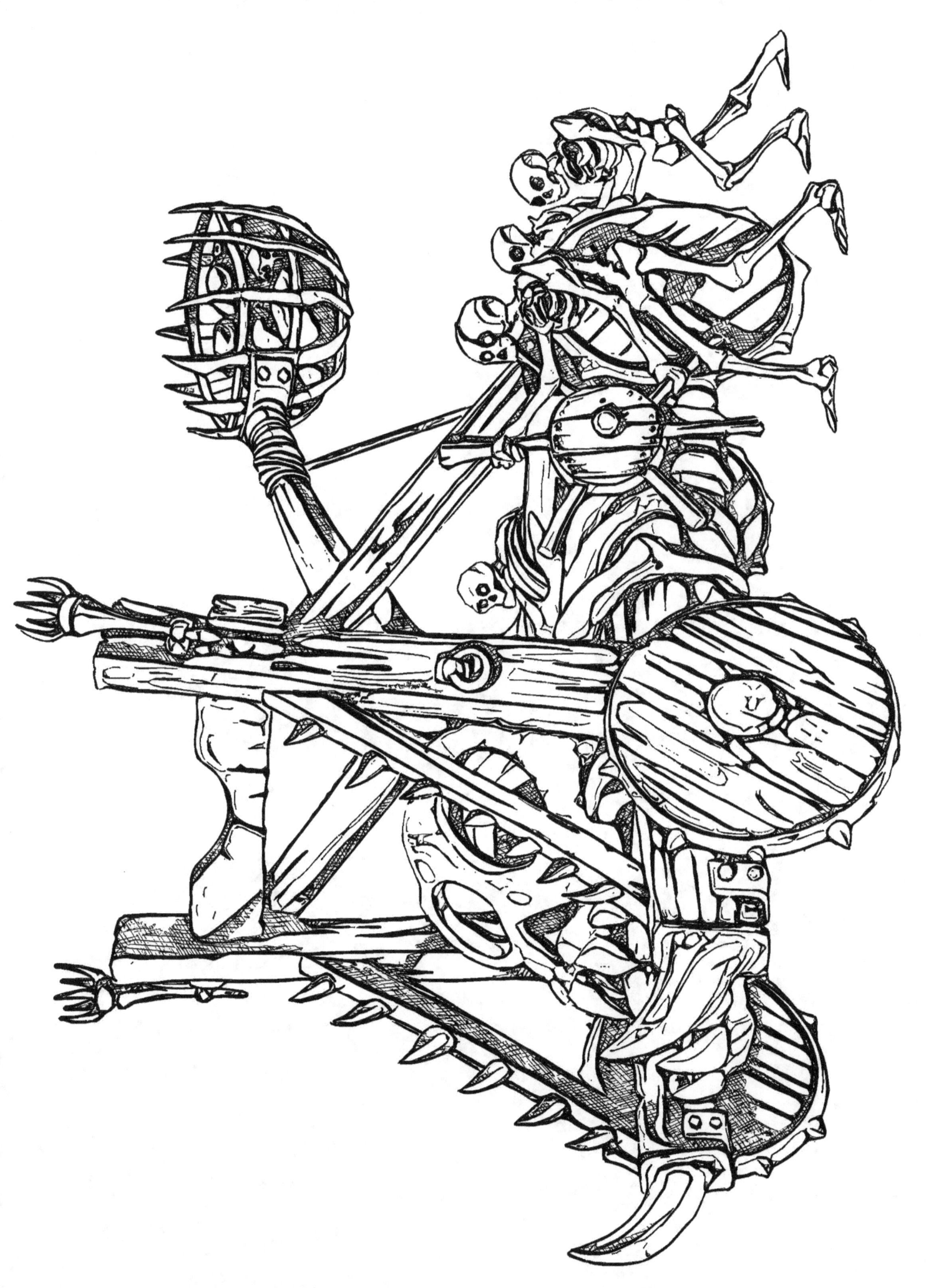

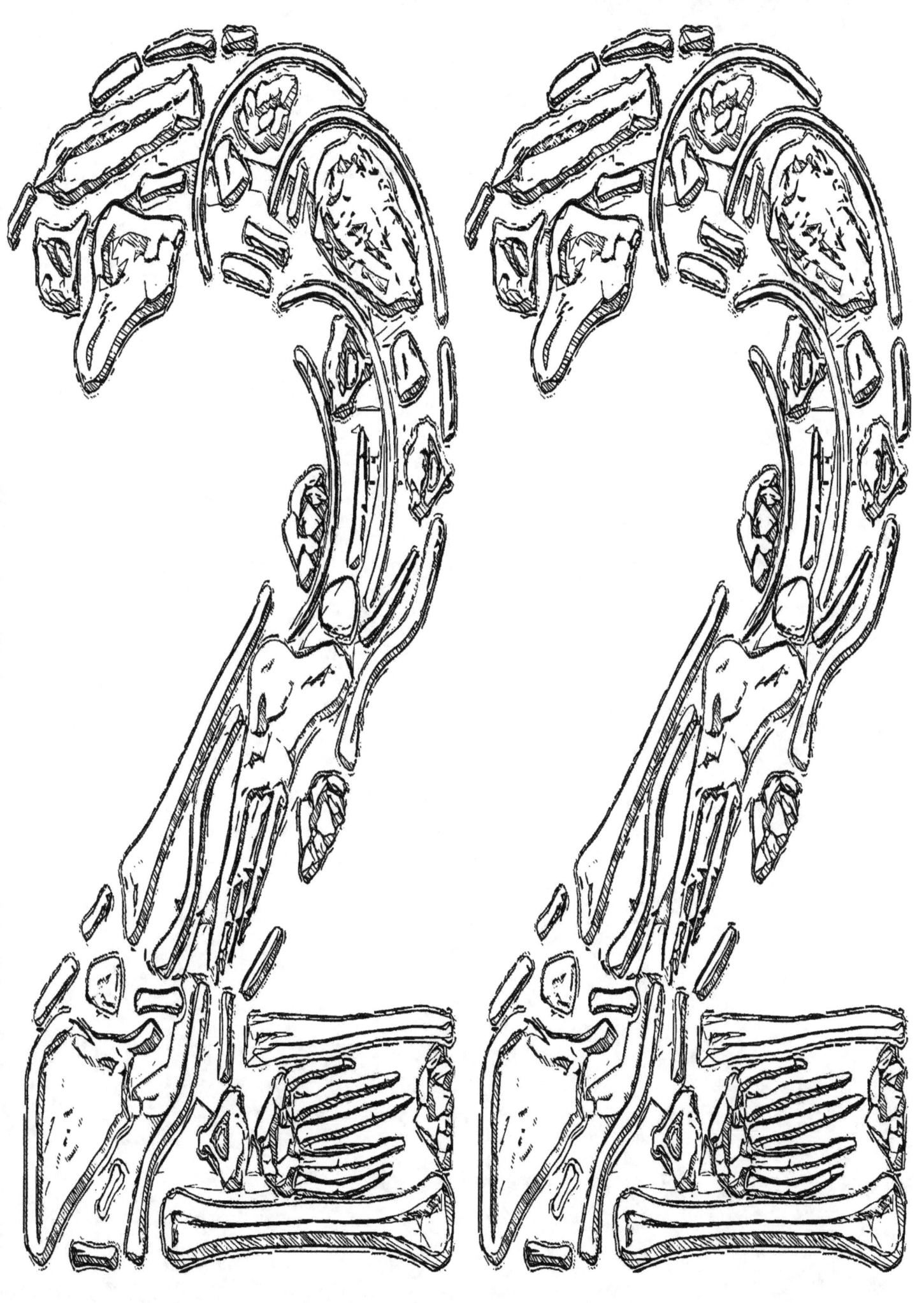

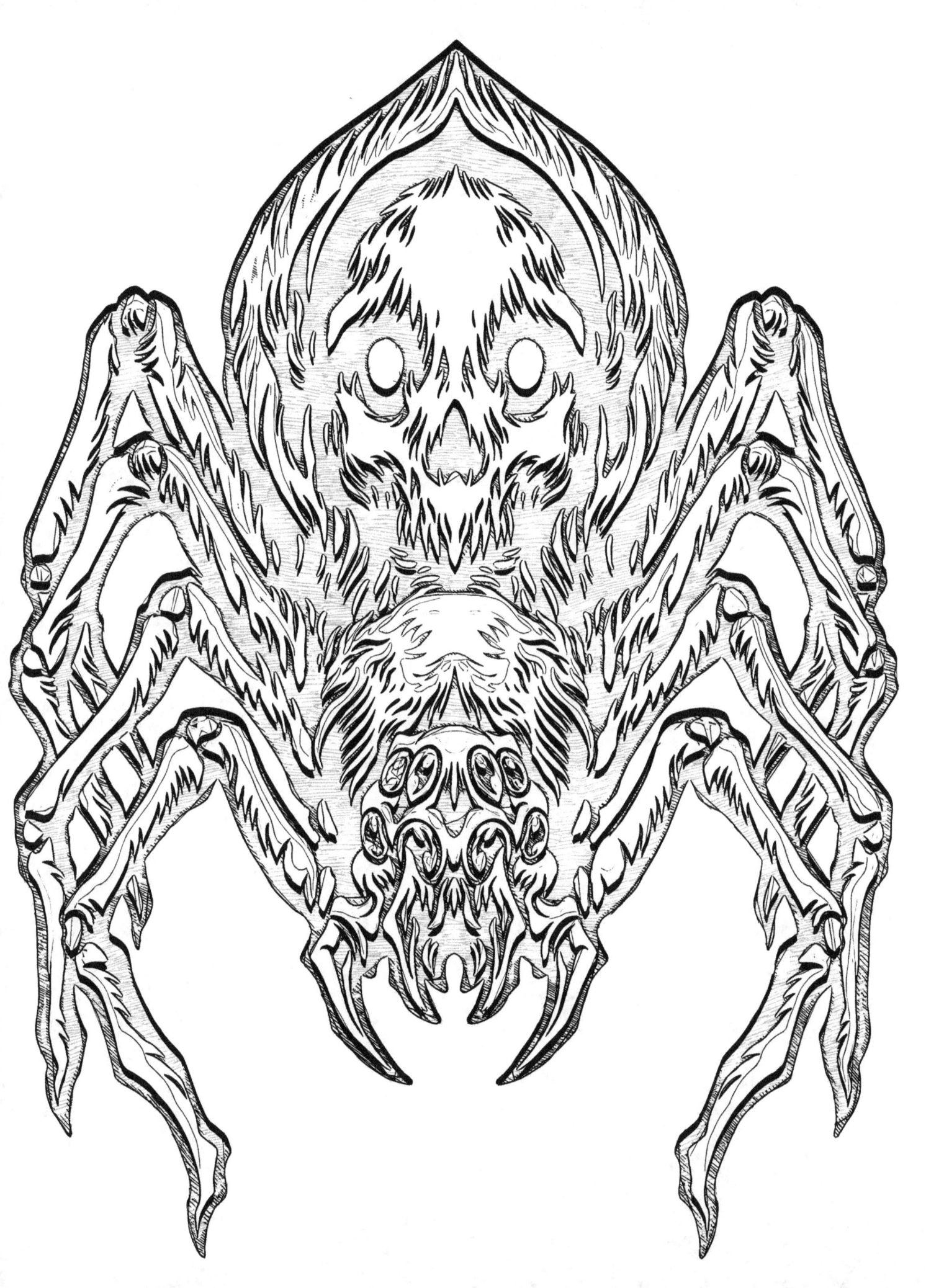

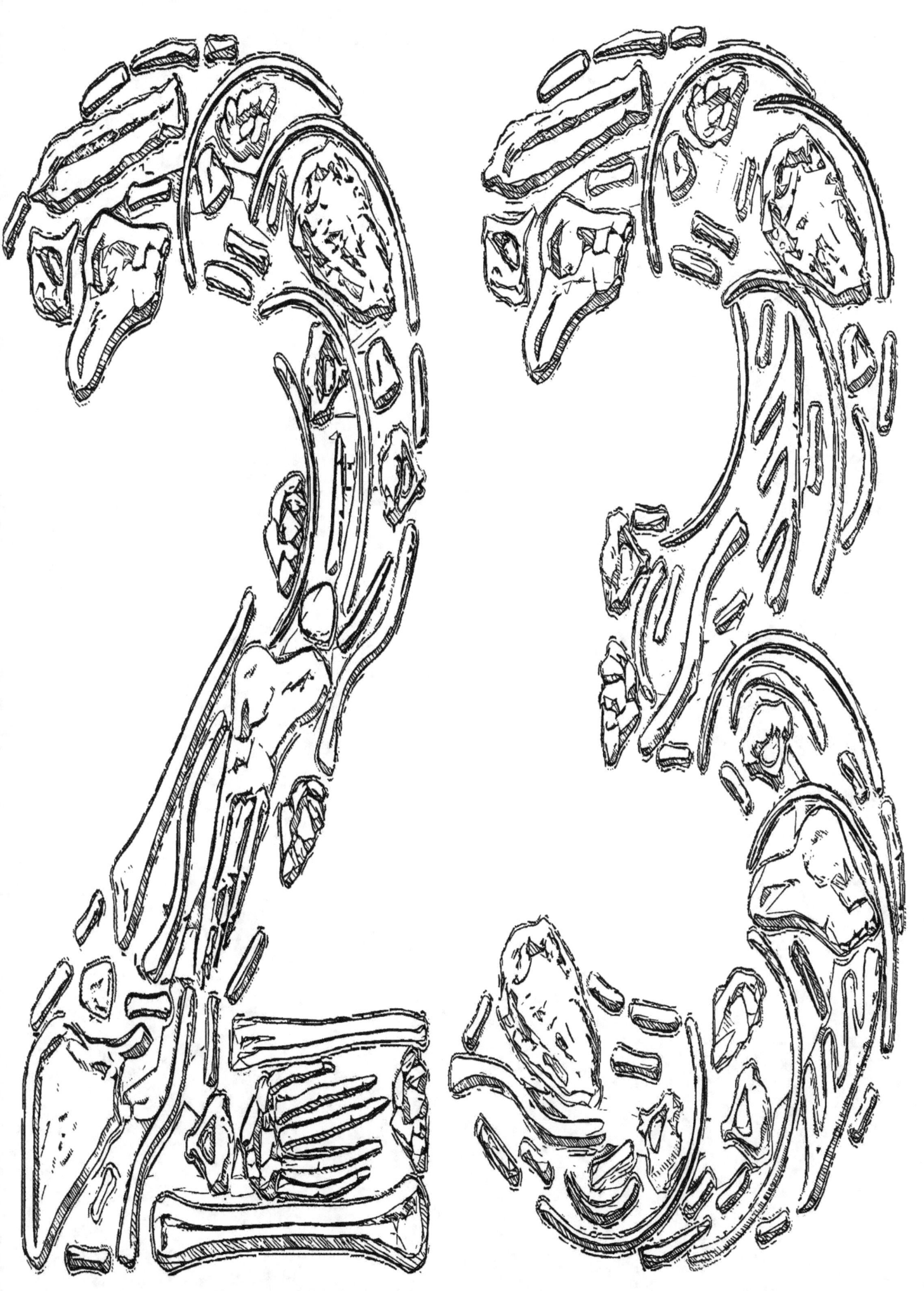

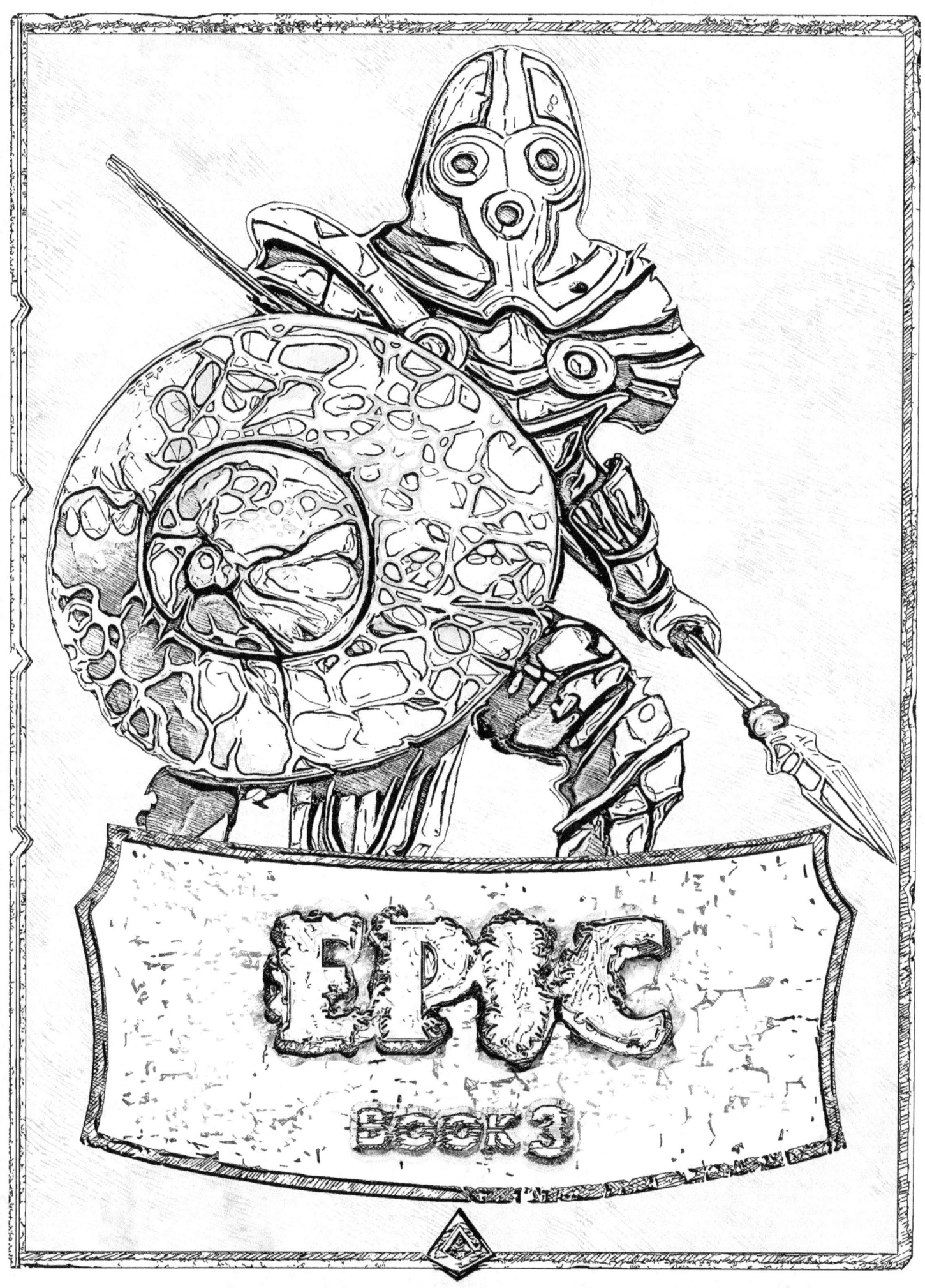

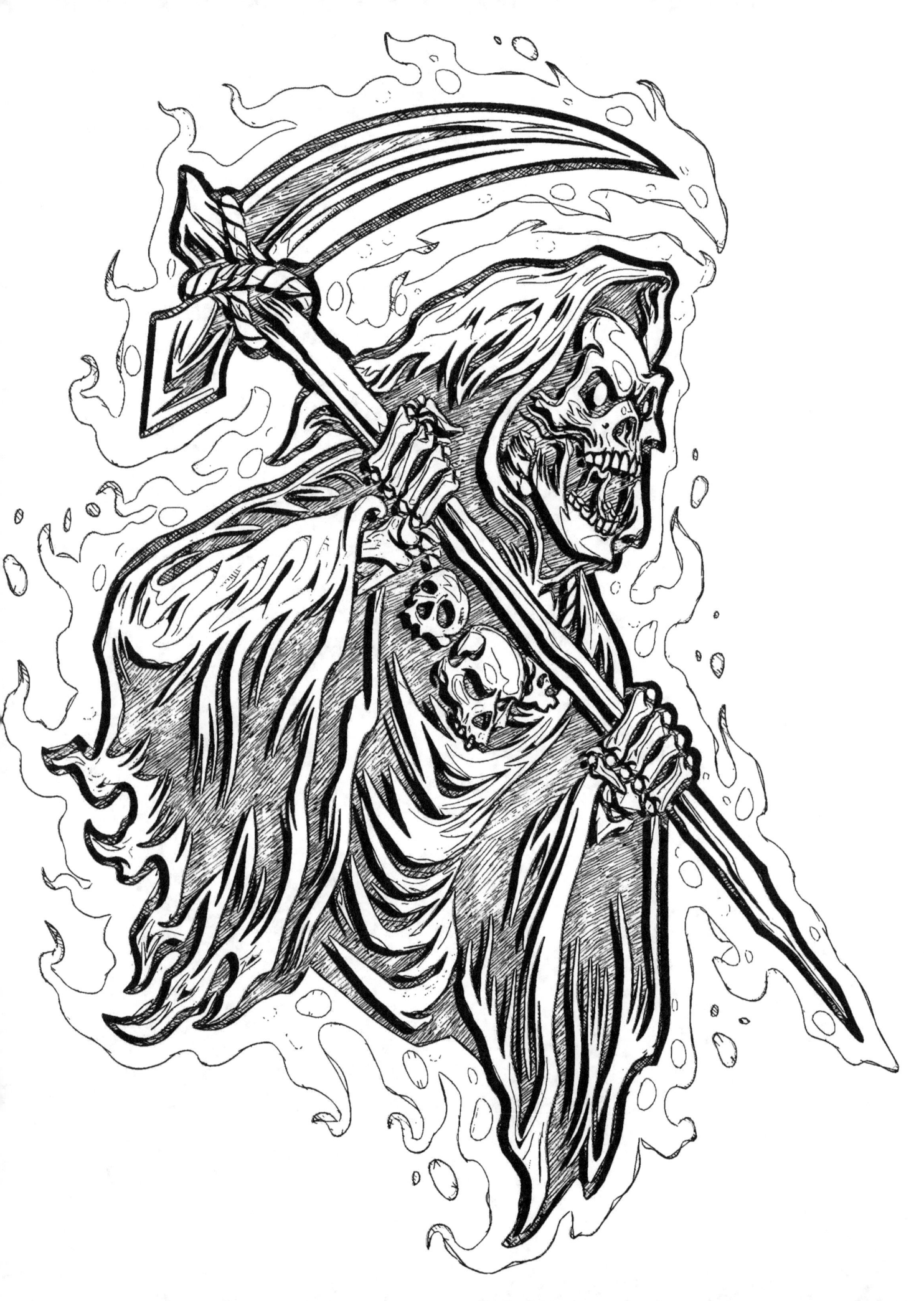

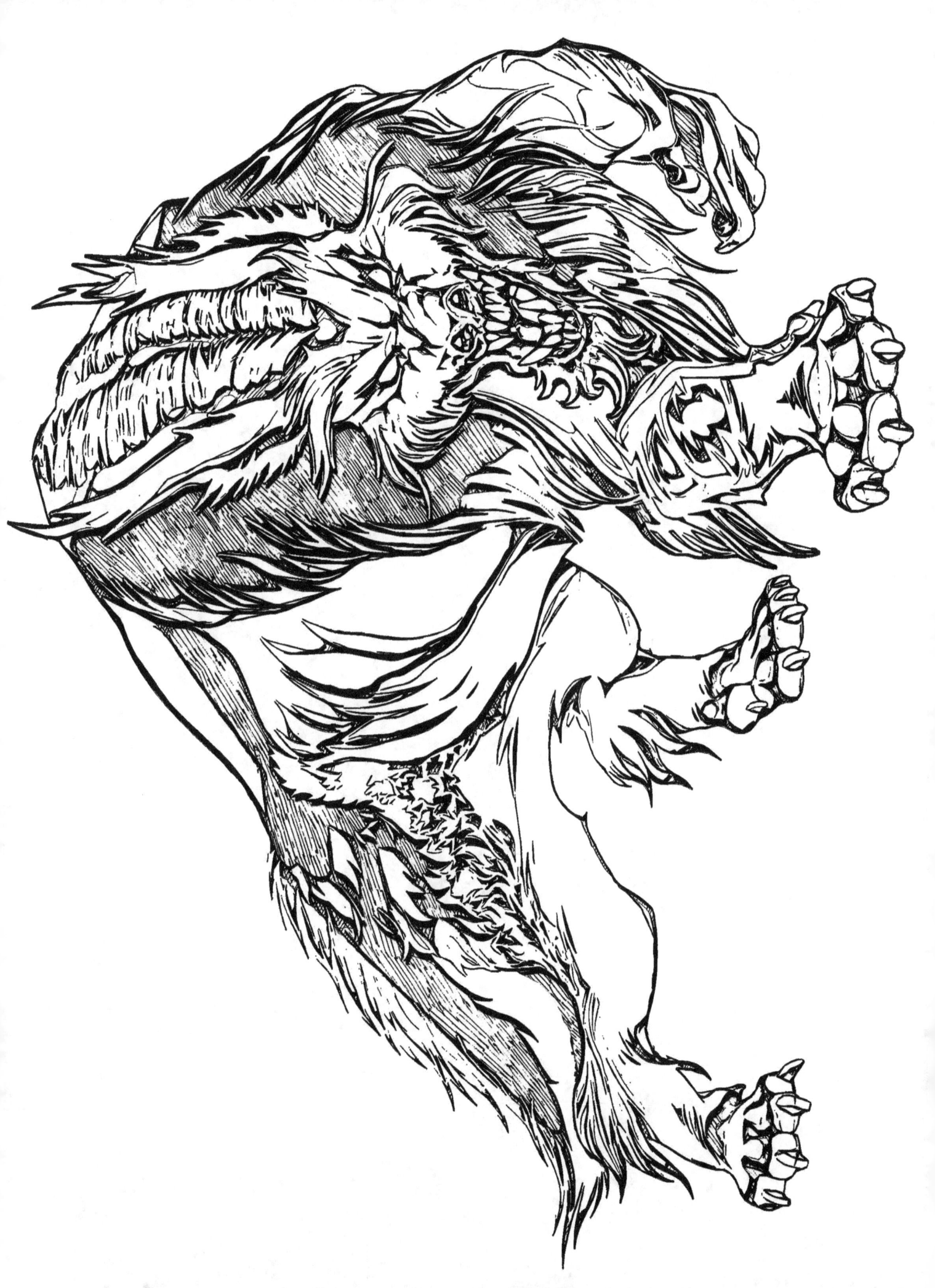

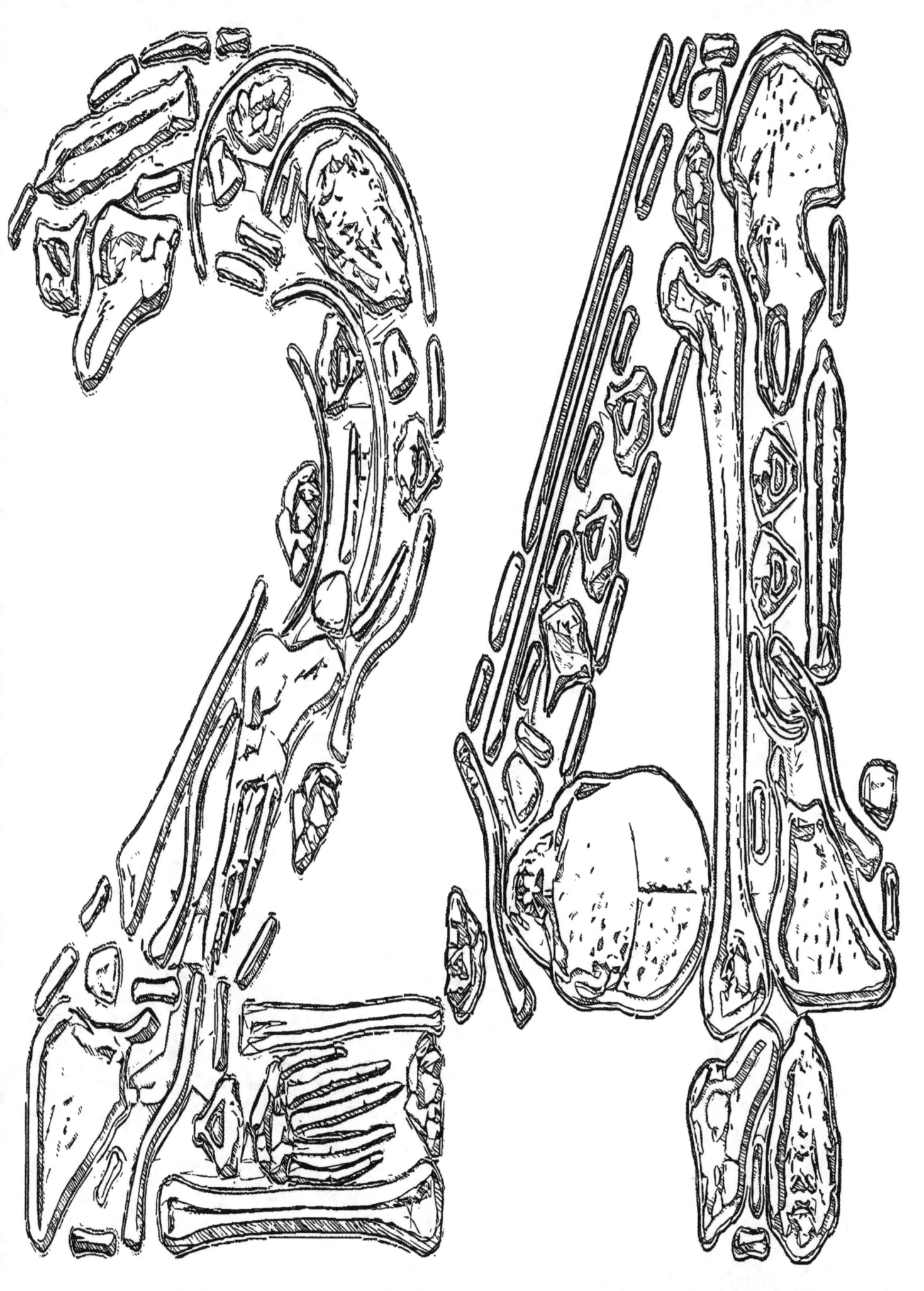

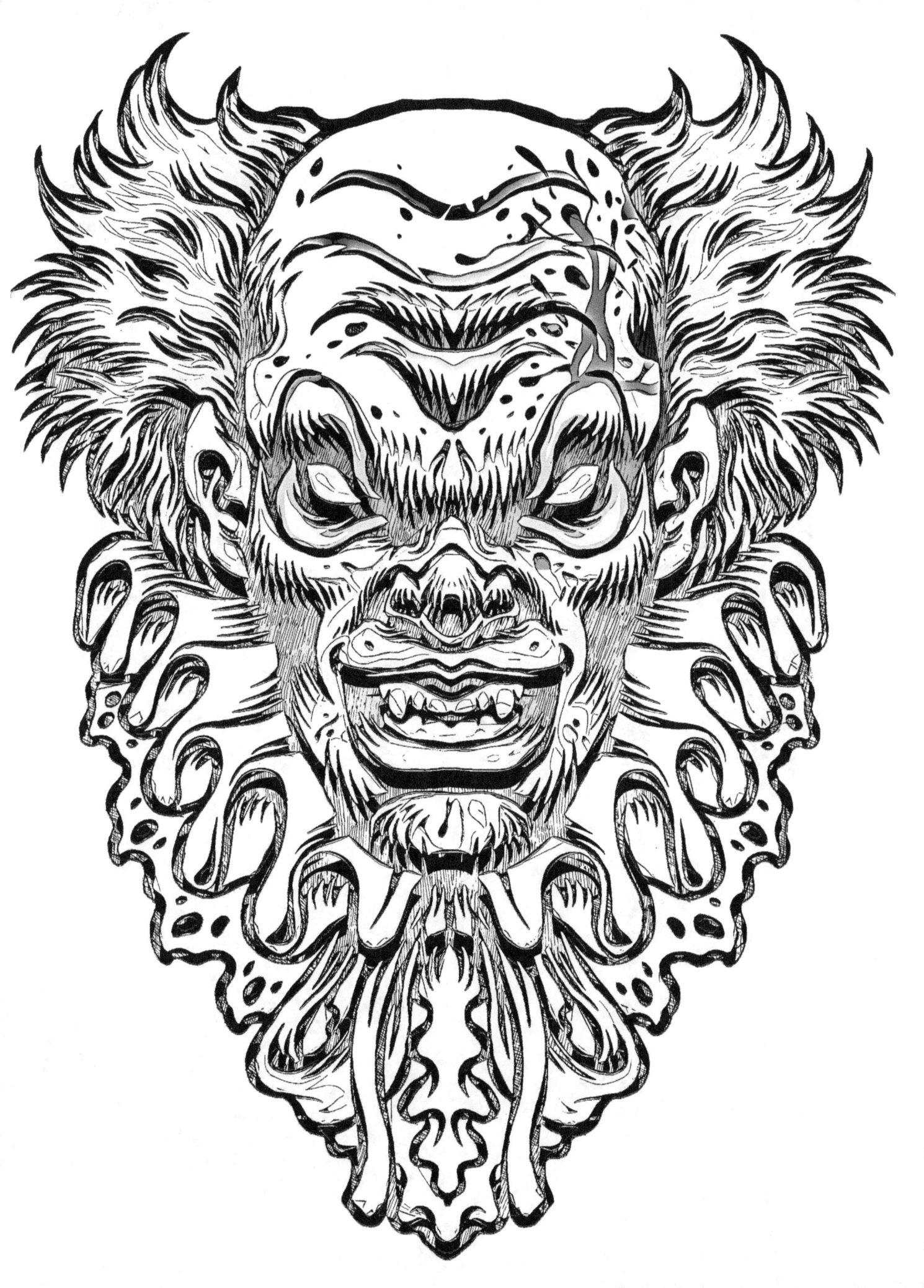

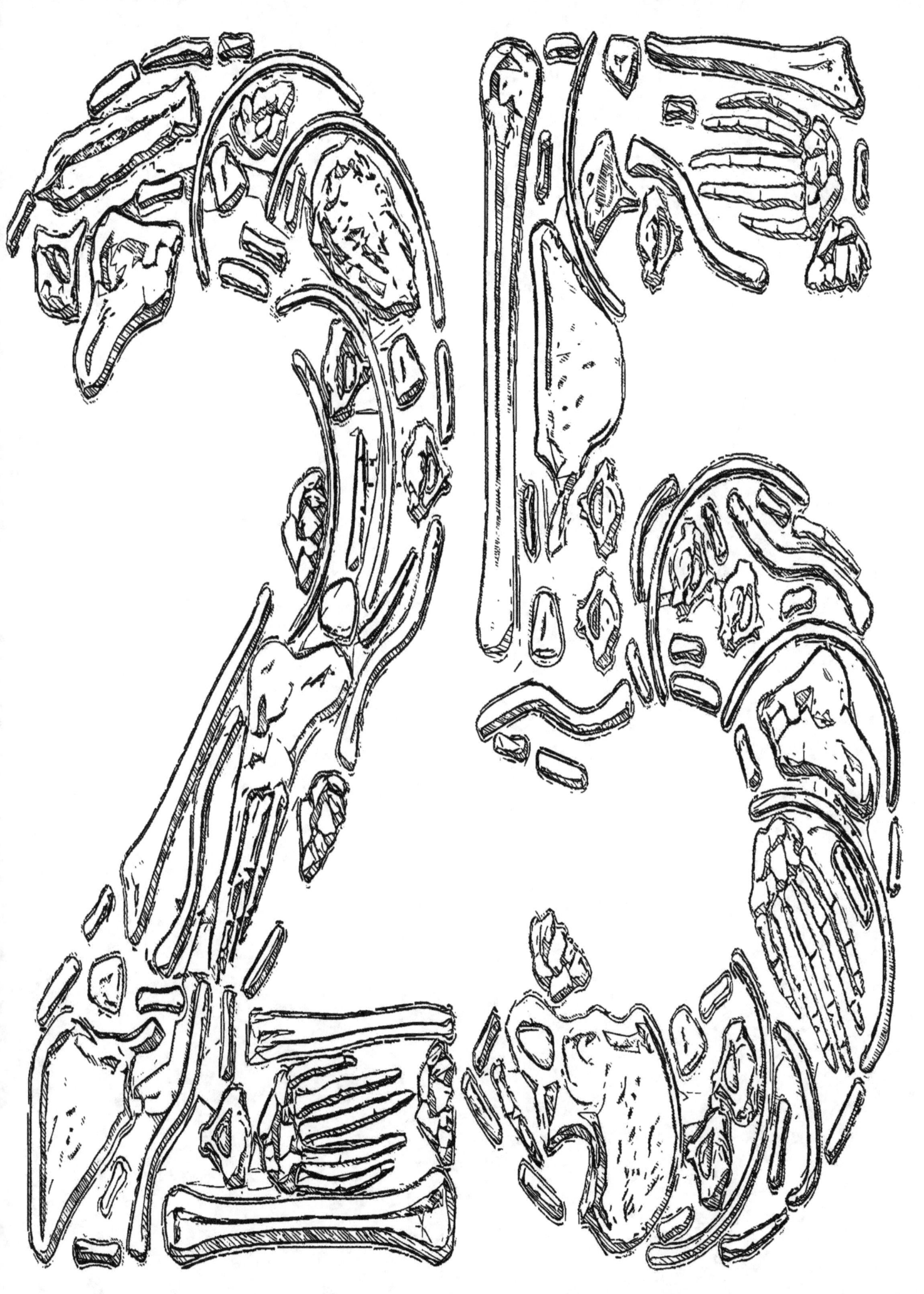

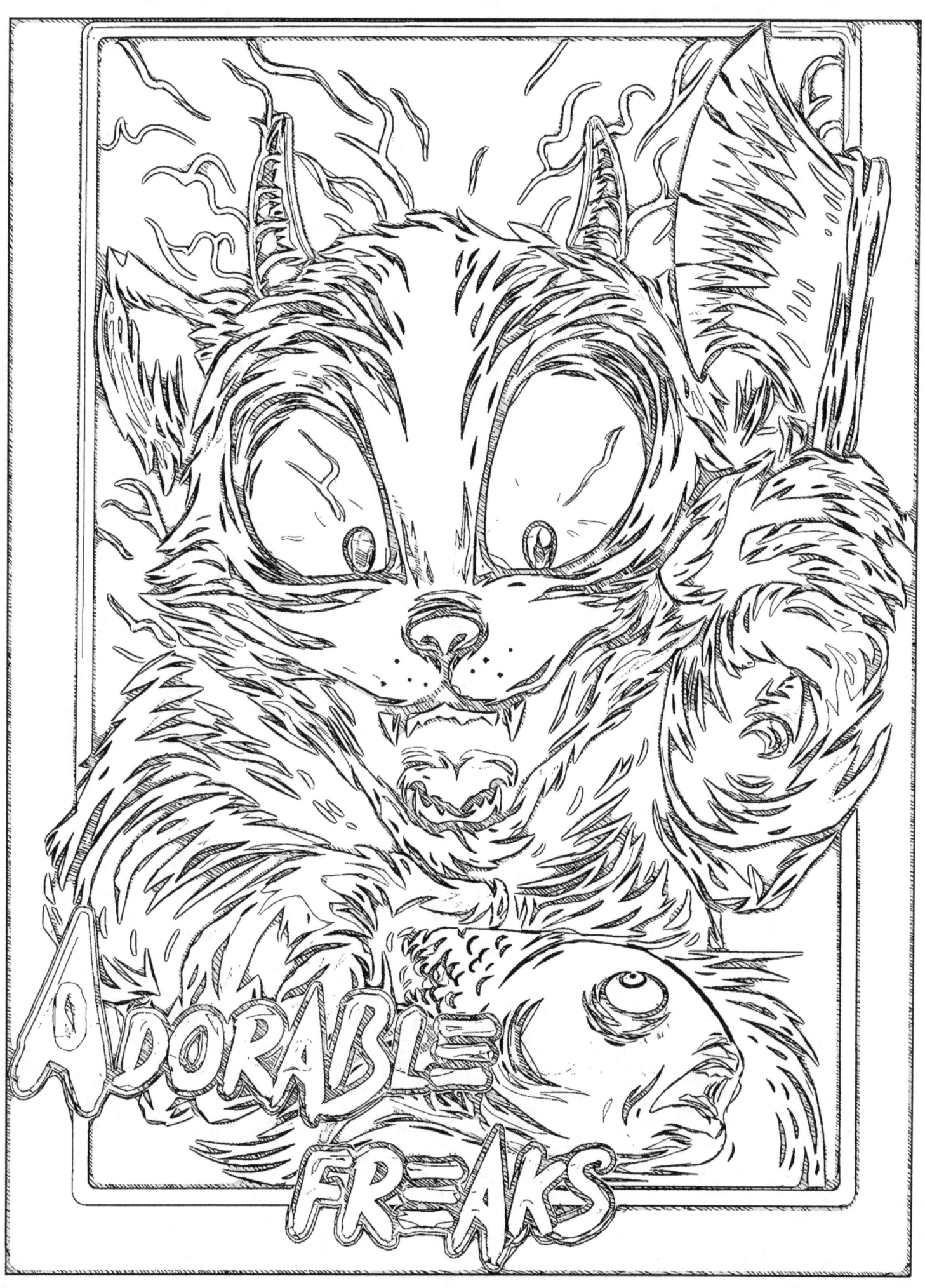

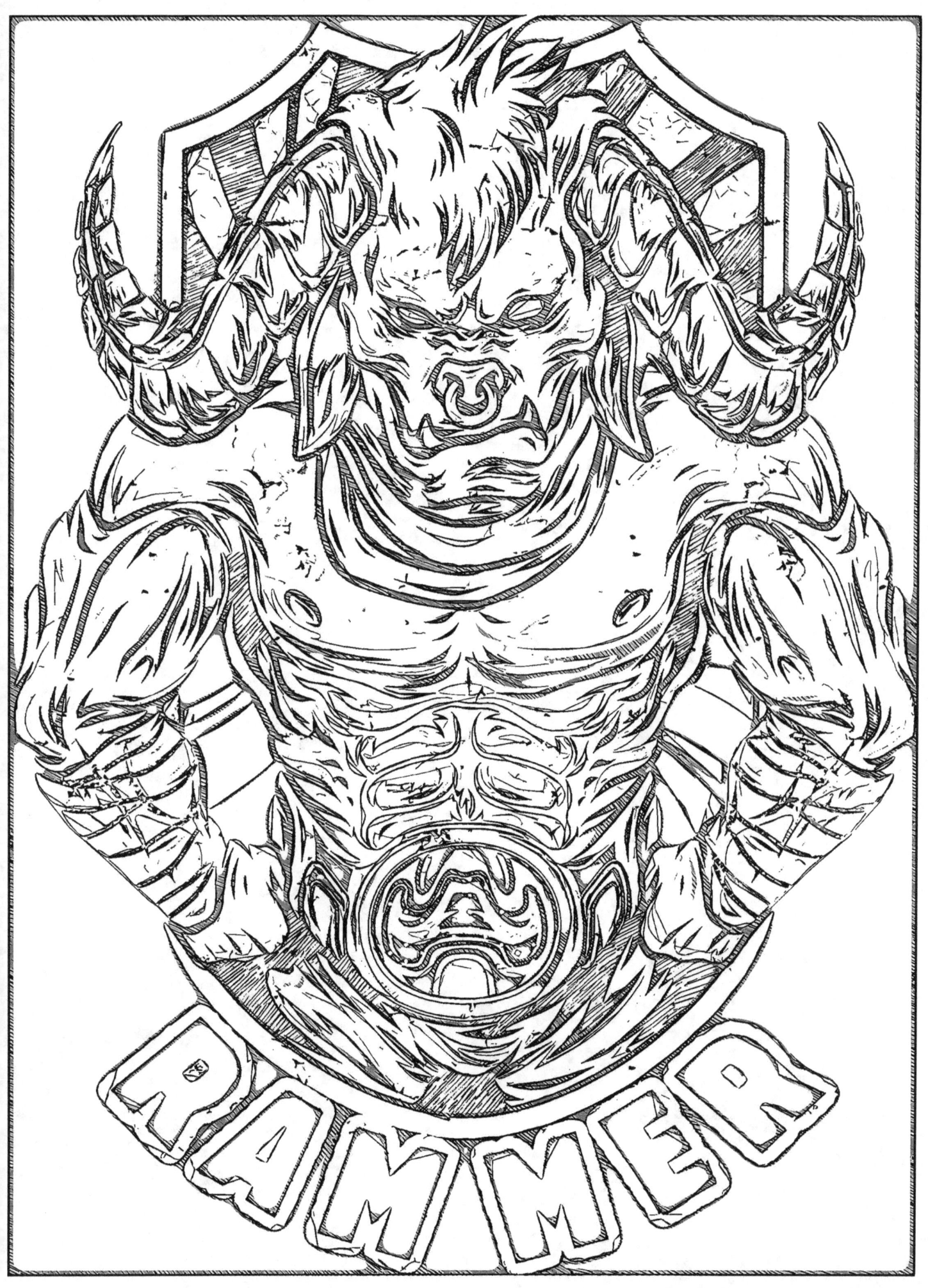

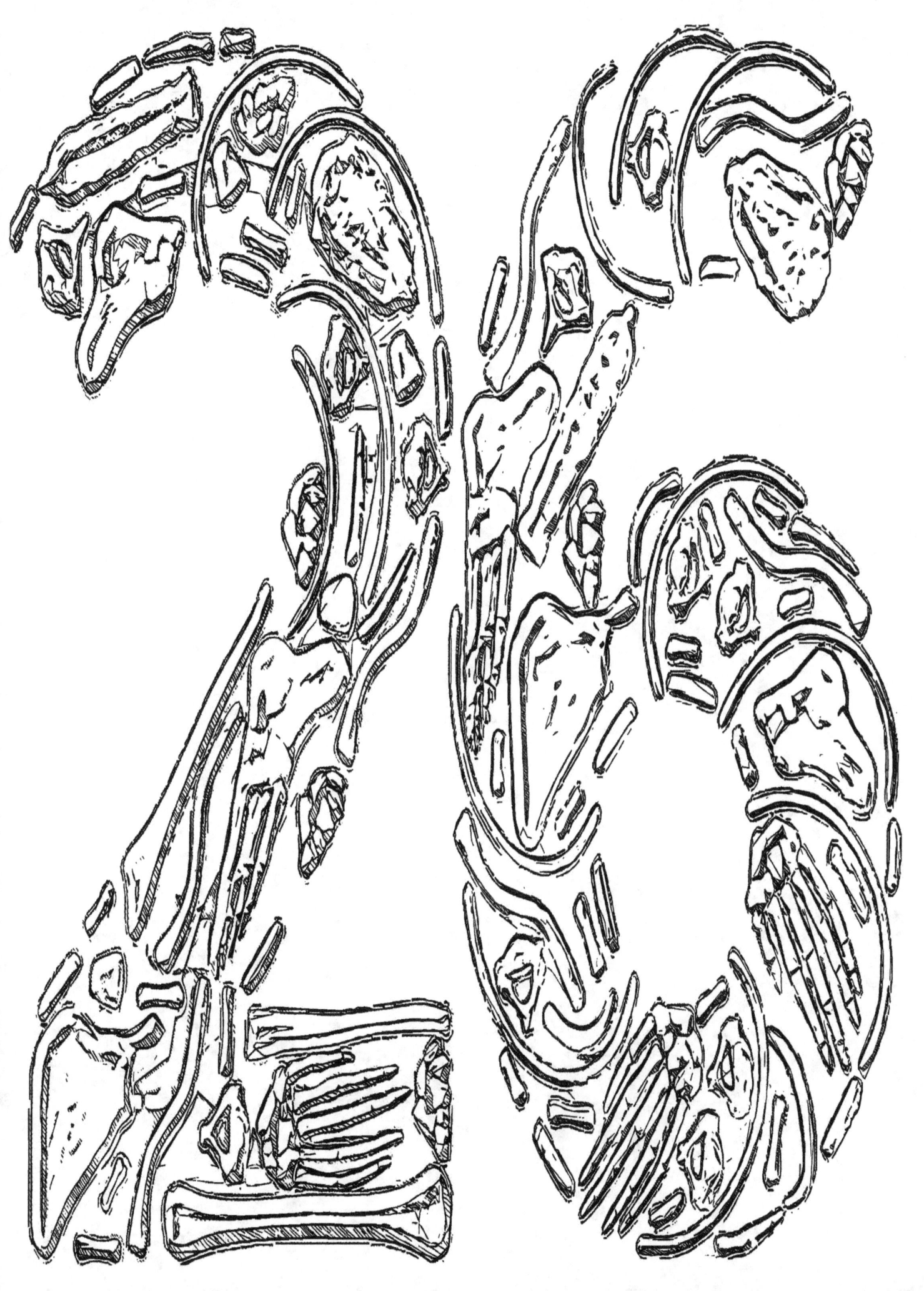

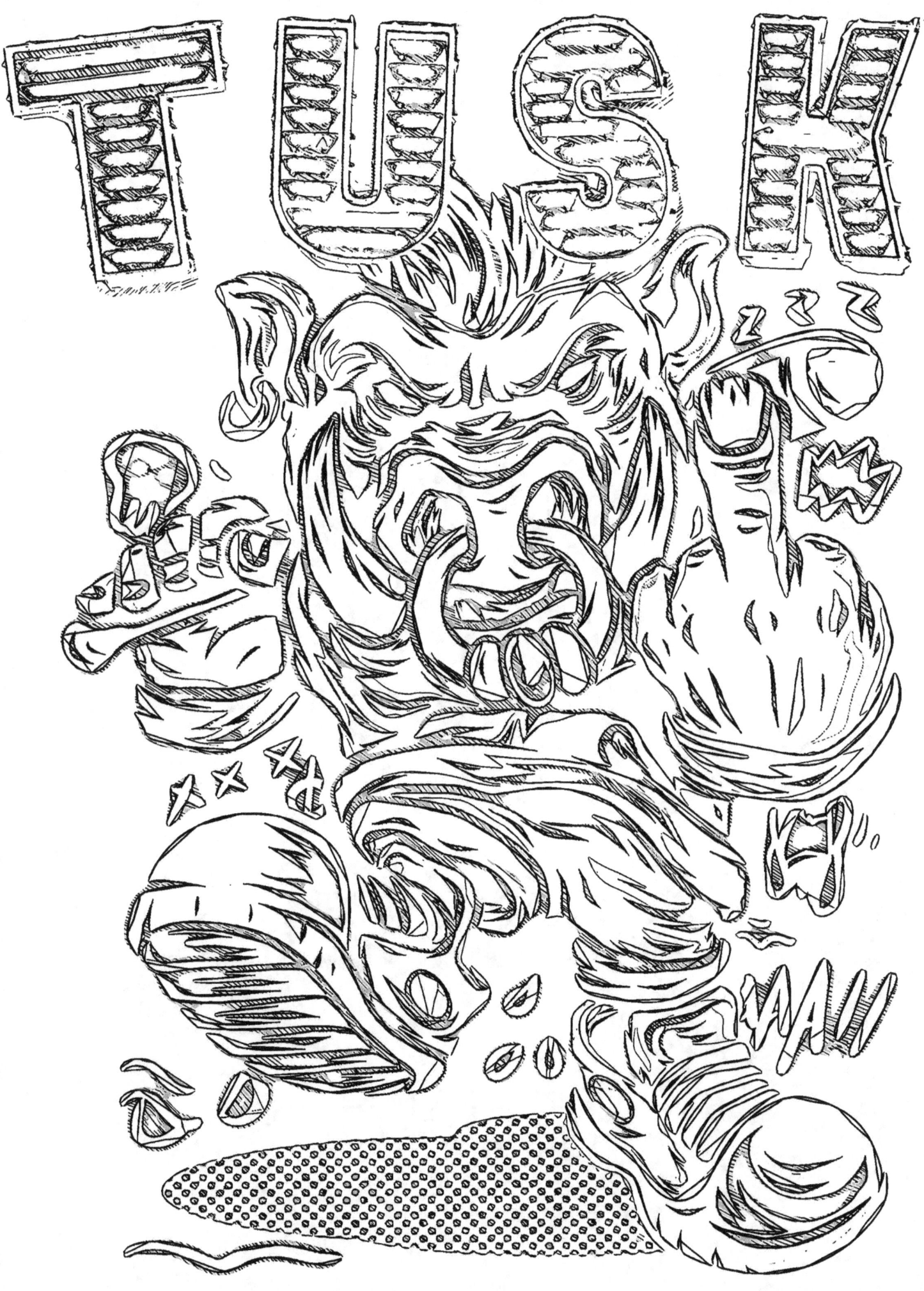

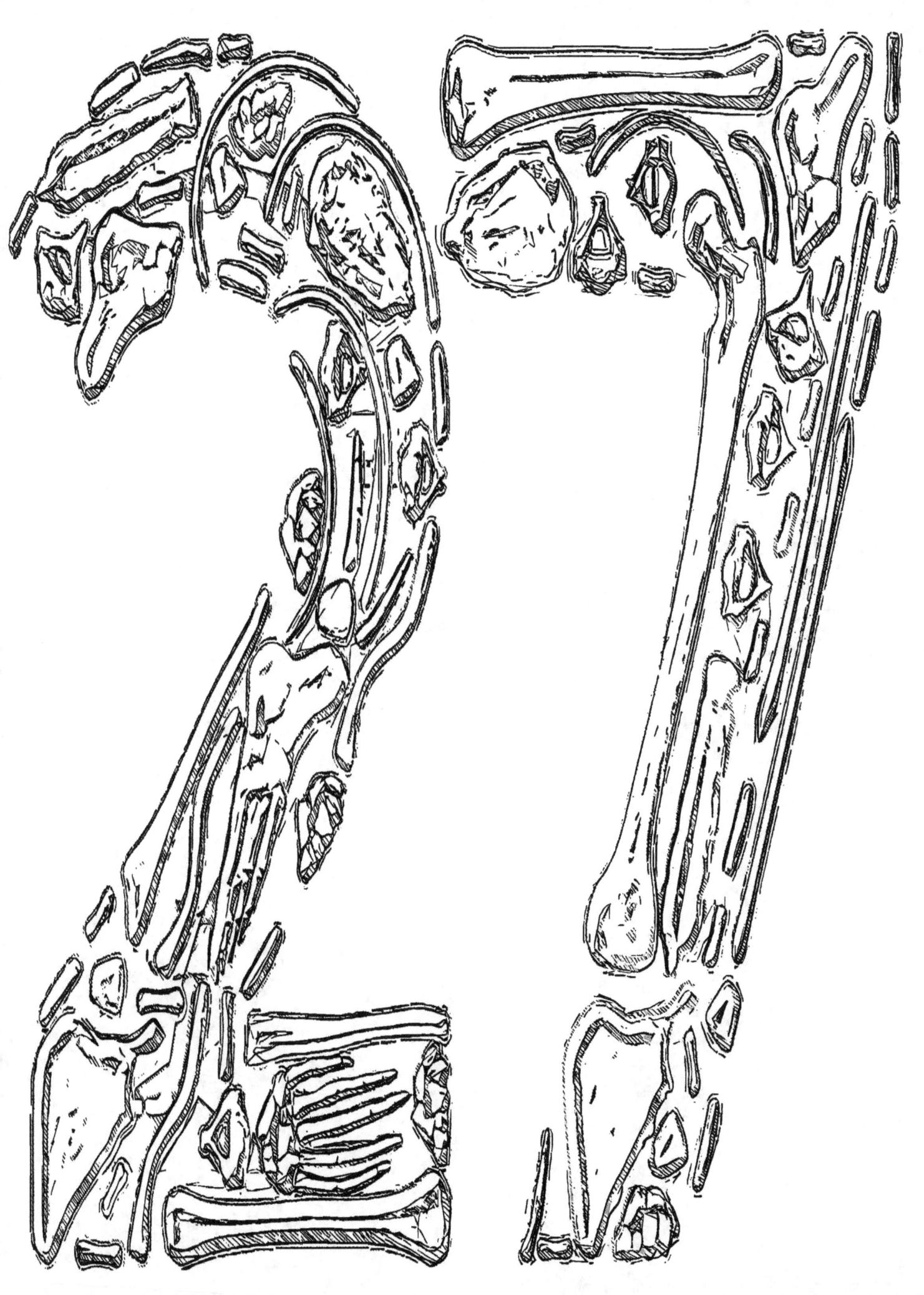

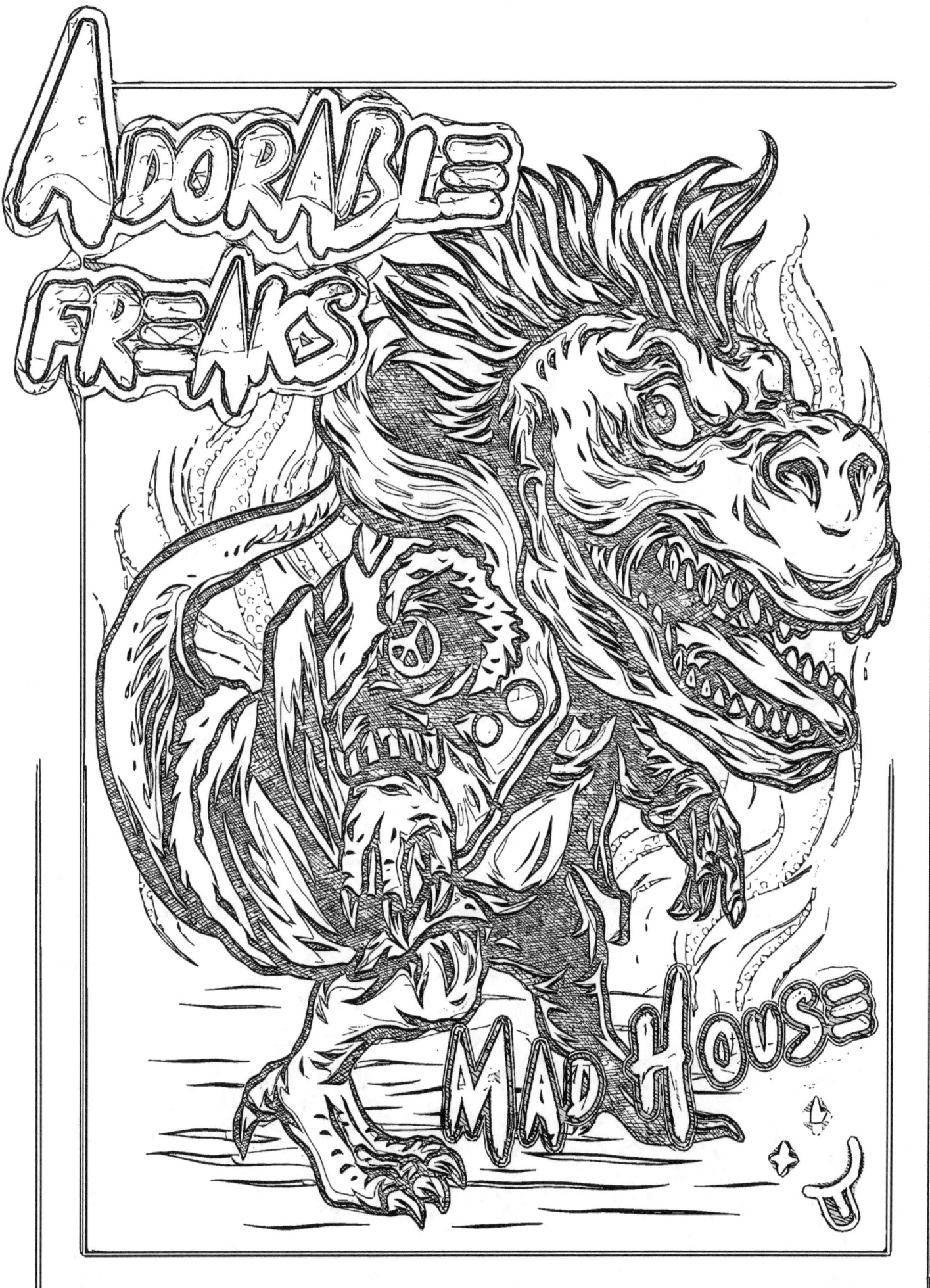

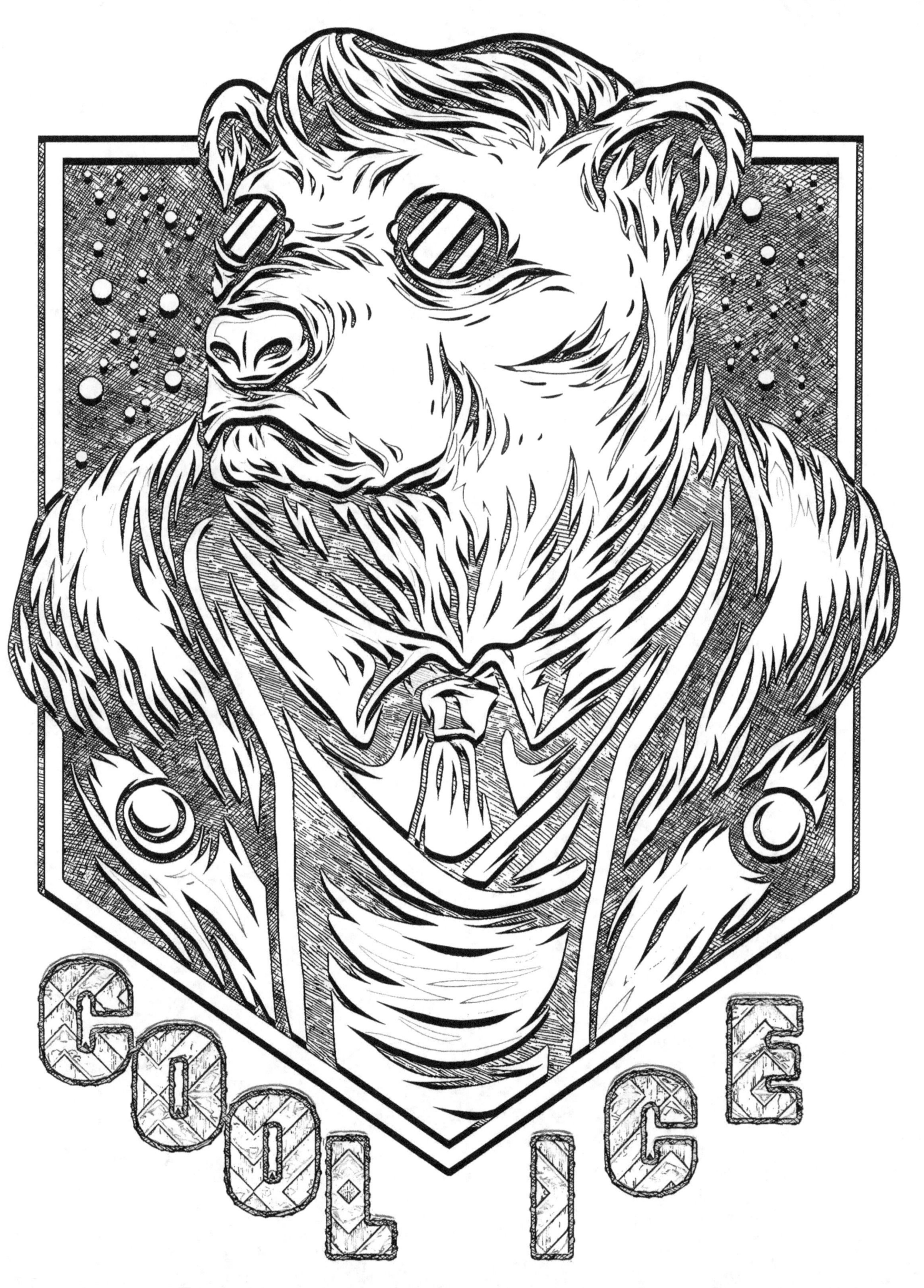

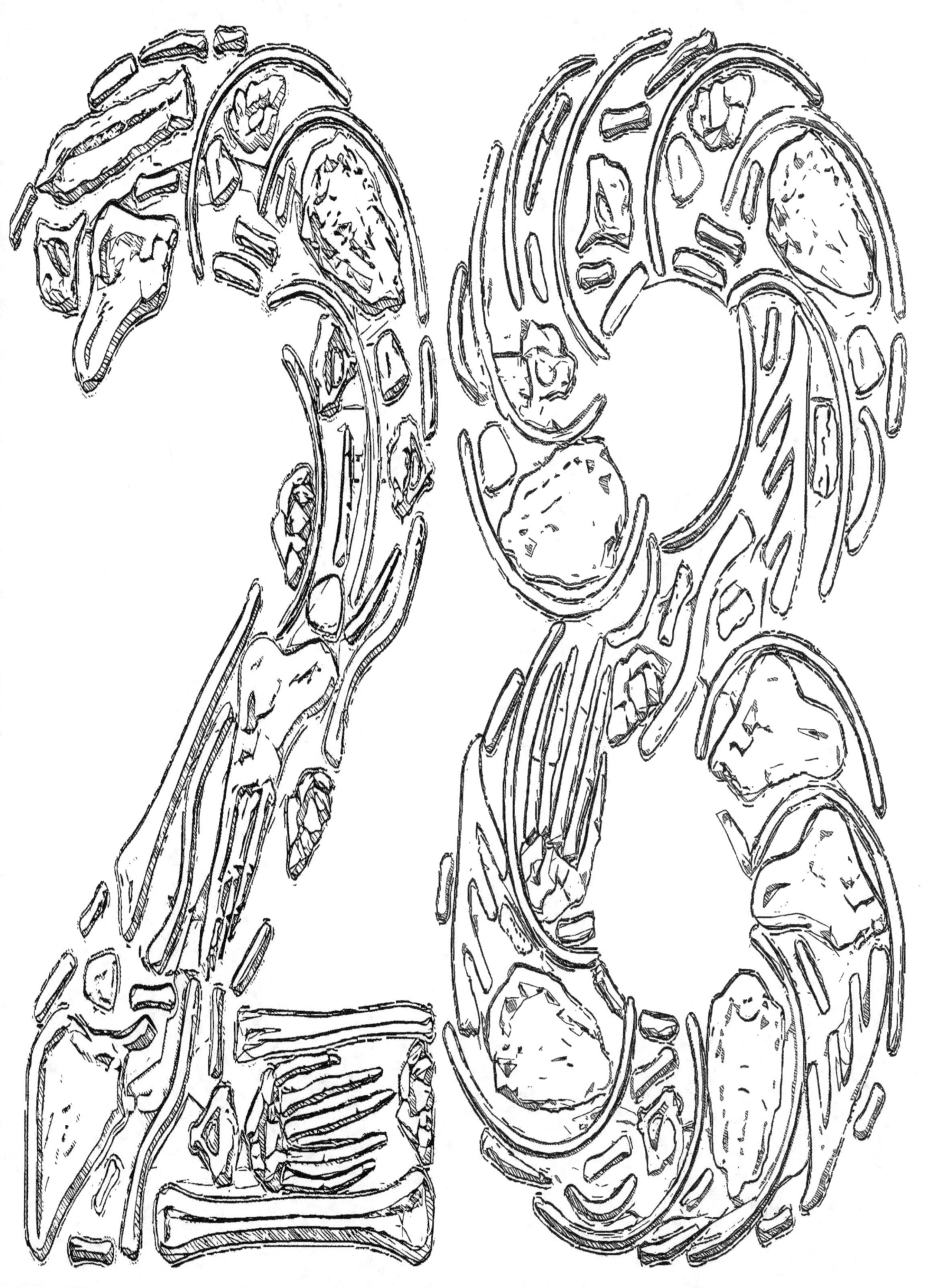

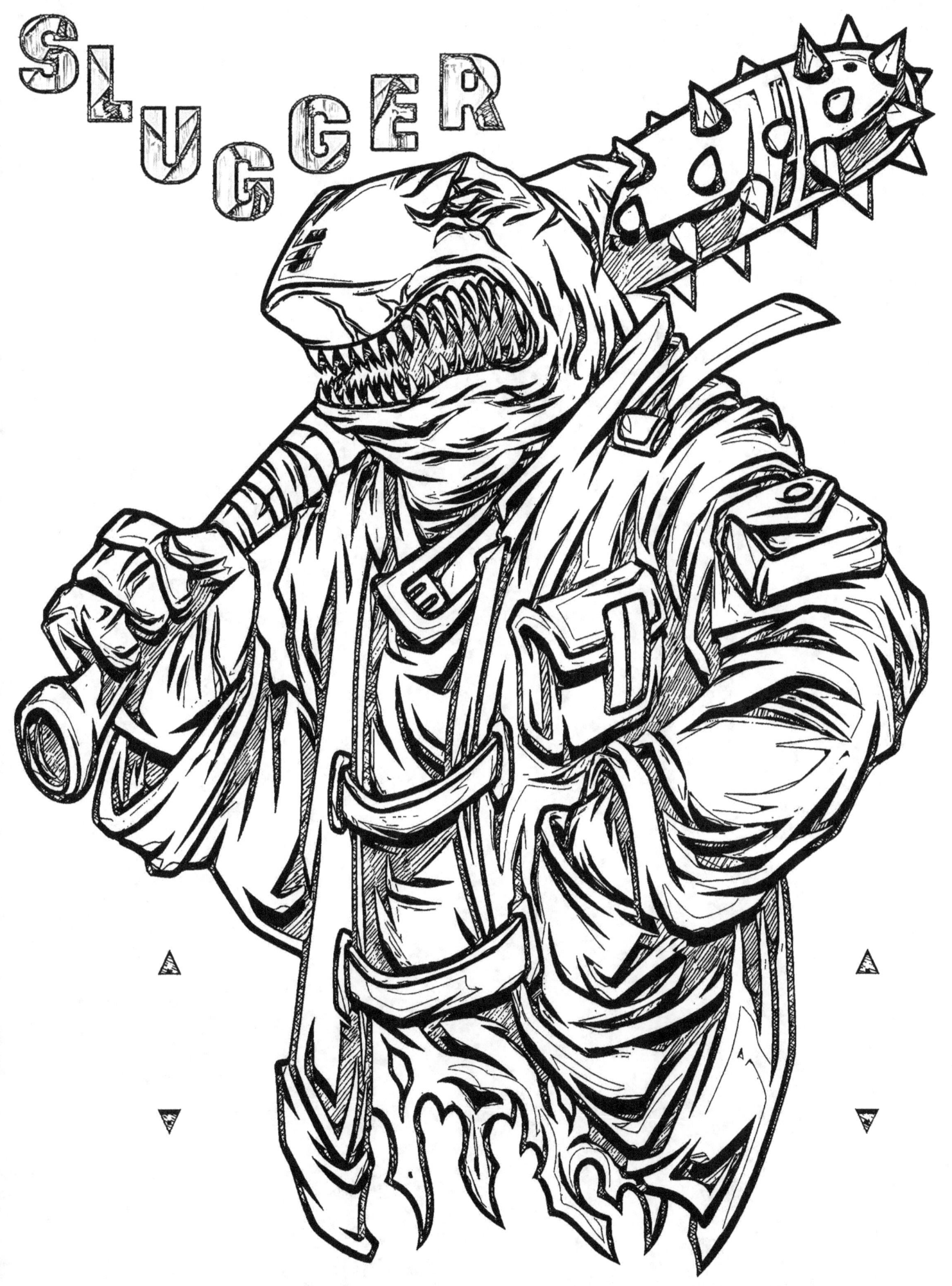

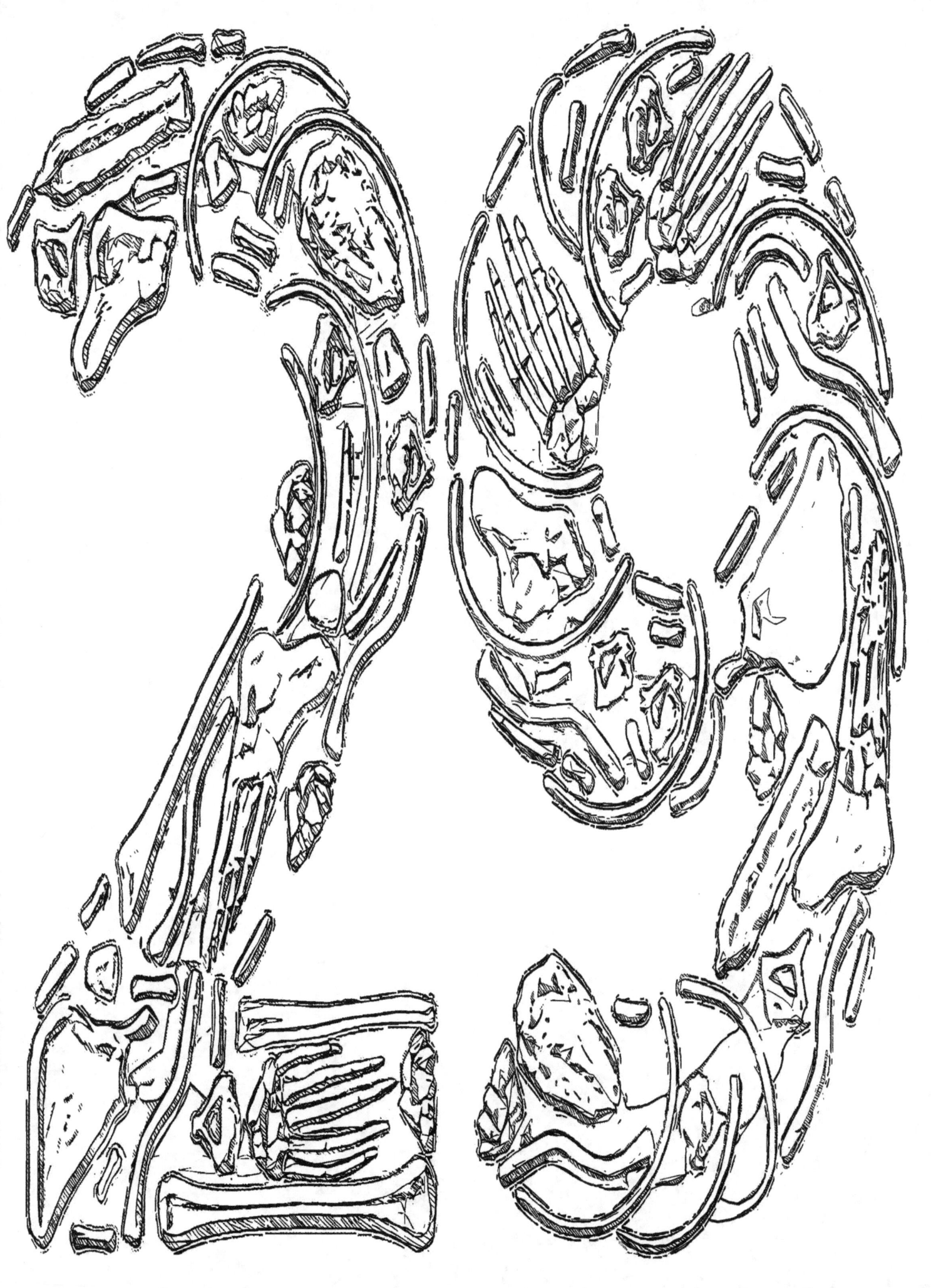

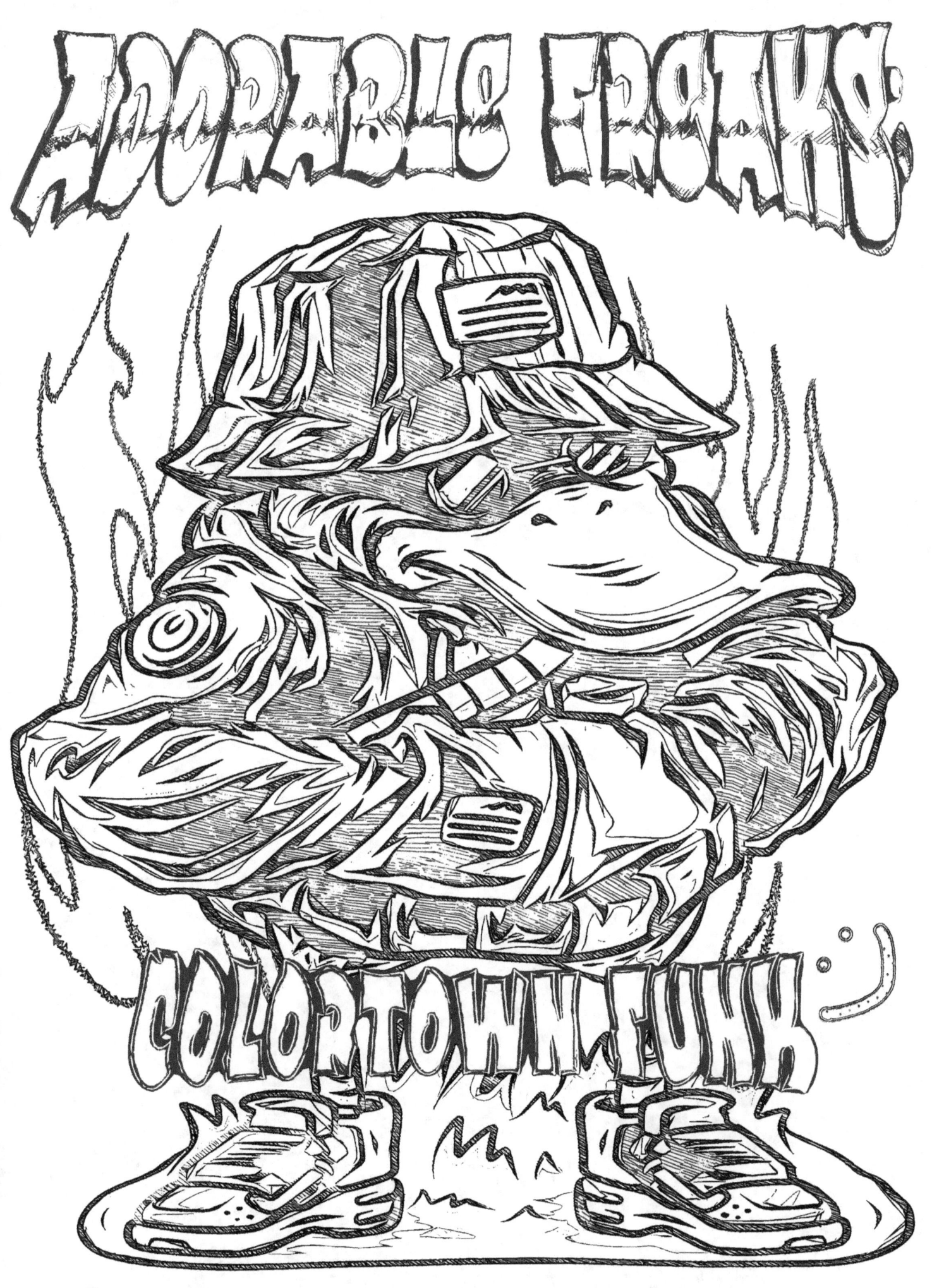

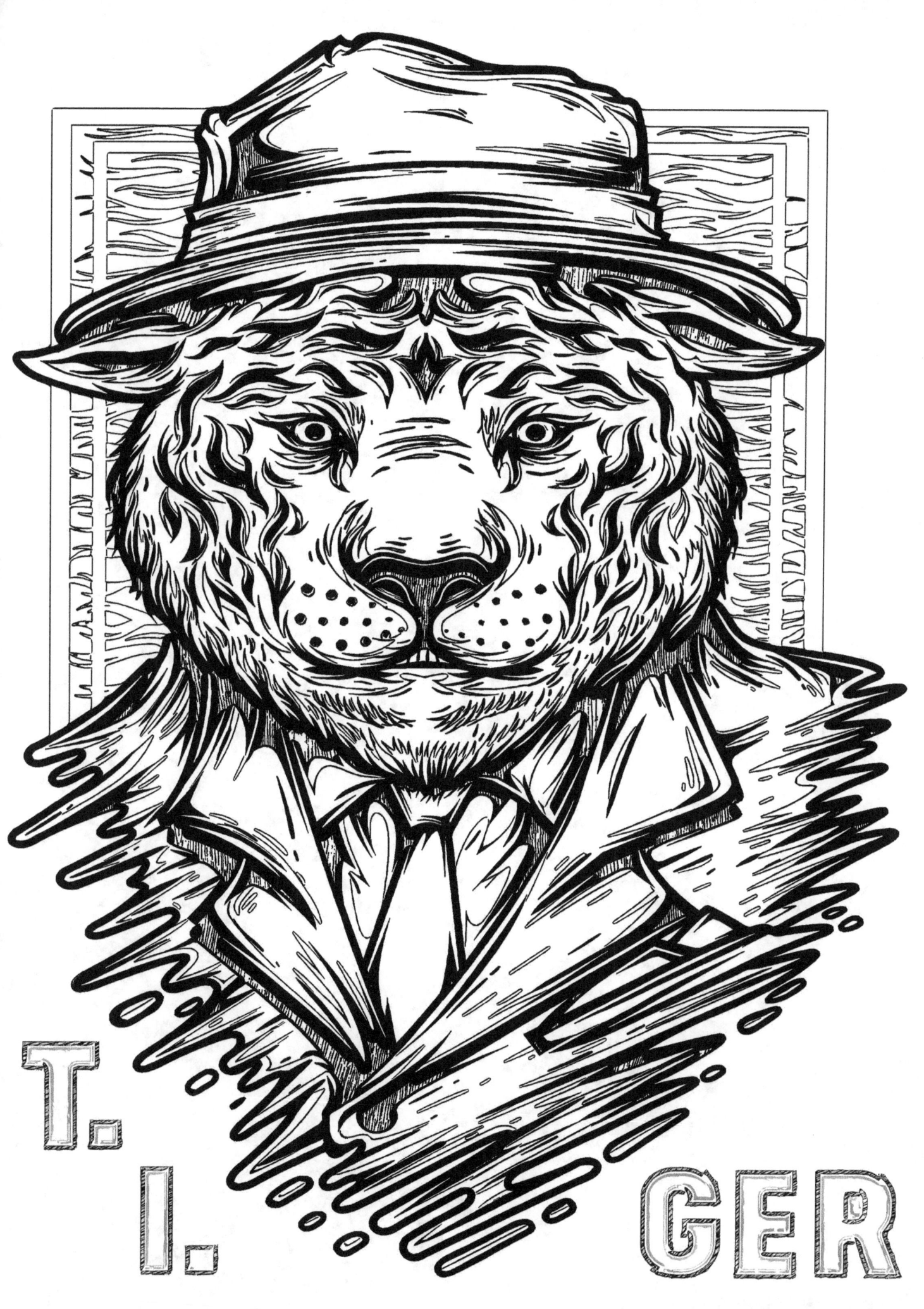

T. I. GER

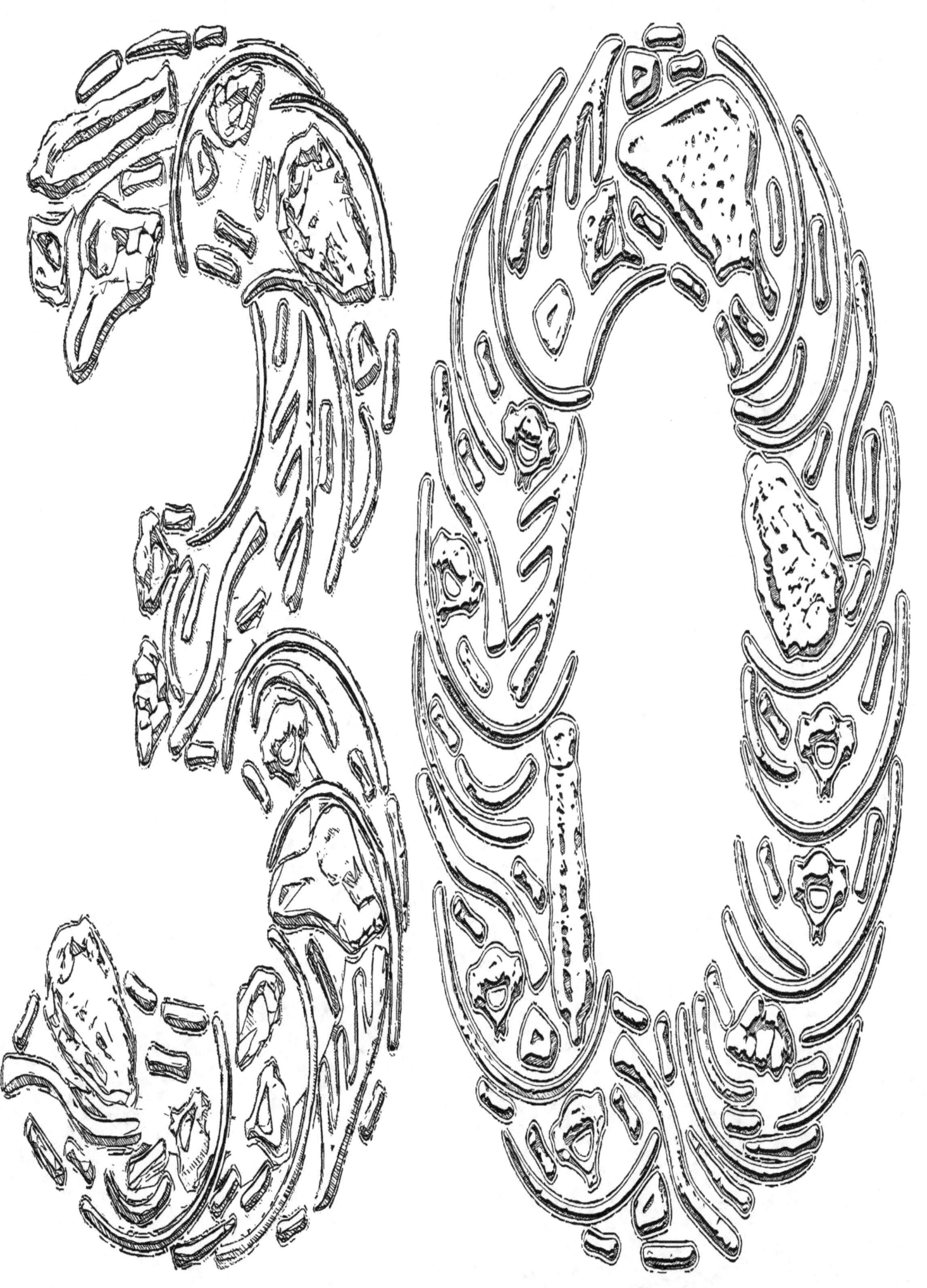

# AMAZON SEARCH TERM: PLASMA HURRICANE

## AMAZON SEARCH CATEGORY: BOOKS

» EPIC

» COMBINES TWO BOOKS:

EPIC

EPIC:
BOOK 2

» ADORABLE
FREAKS:
MAD HOUSE

« EPIC:
BOOK 2

« ADORABLE
FREAKS

« COMBINES TWO
BOOKS:

ADORABLE
FREAKS

ADORABLE
FREAKS:
MAD HOUSE

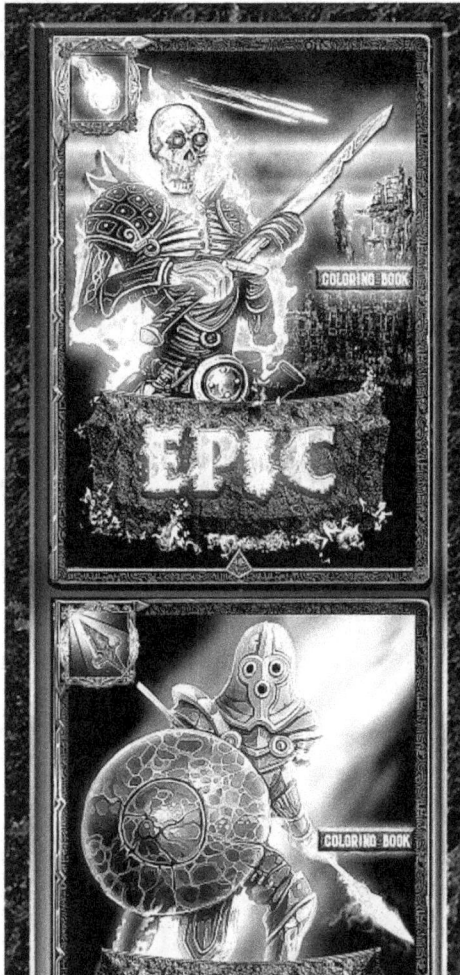
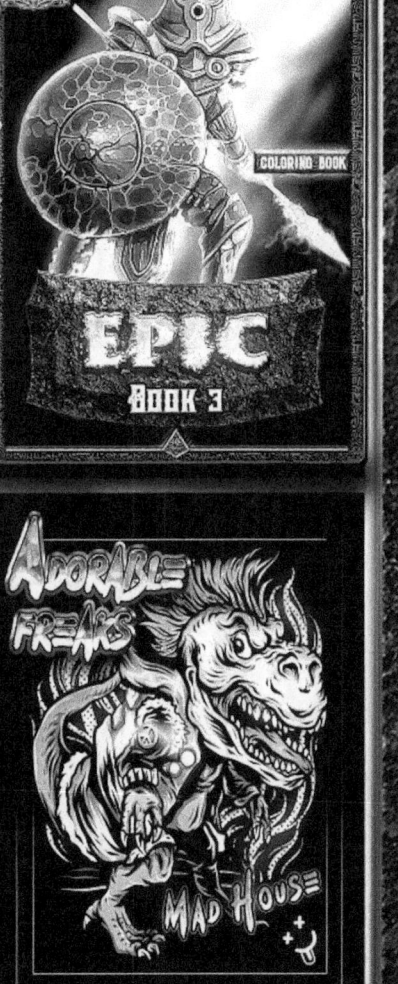

www.ingramcontent.com/pod-product-compliance
Lightning Source LLC
Chambersburg PA
CBHW081725220526
45468CB00008B/1975